Revisited

RONALD RUSSEL

Copyright © 2023 by Ronald Russel

ISBN: 978-1-77883-088-4 (Paperback)

All rights reserved. No part of this publication may be reproduced, distributed, or transmitted in any form or by any means, including photocopying, recording, or other electronic or mechanical methods, without the prior written permission of the publisher, except in the case brief quotations embodied in critical reviews and other noncommercial uses permitted by copyright law.

The views expressed in this book are solely those of the author and do not necessarily reflect the views of the publisher, and the publisher hereby disclaims any responsibility for them.

BookSide Press
877-741-8091
www.booksidepress.com
orders@booksidepress.com

Introduction

This is the second writing of the book 'A Life So Good'. Much of the first book has not been altered; however flesh has been added to the bones, hopefully enabling the reader to experience the deeper emotions experienced by me during this wonderful but at times terrifying journey through life.

This book is loosely based on my life experiences, most of the events did happen but the settings may have been changed.

One of the reasons I am writing this is to draw attention to, and give a firsthand view on what life was like among some indigenous peoples and those society might like to call 'No hopers', that small army who trudged the outback roads in search of work which paid little more than food and tobacco, many to whom this country owes a debt of gratitude for the labour and ingenuity supplied by these, dare I say, pioneers.

I would also like to mention that I'm not proportioning any blame here; it is my firm belief that we always do our best with whatever knowledge we have in each moment and cannot judge past actions in hindsight.

Black bastard, yellafella, white trash, were the derogatory terms which surrounded or accompanied me through much of my life, and I first heard these terms when I was about fifteen years old while living in a small coal mining town west of Sydney in New South Wales.

Rita my sister was tall for her twelve years, and like most of the other girls in our street, very much the tomboy, Rita always played cricket and football with us, and loved climbing mountains. Ellie the friend she brought home lived with her mum, dad and older brother Robert in a simple home a few blocks from us in a street that ran along the railway line, this street was bordered on one side by homes, while the other climbed steeply up to a rocky topped mountain, and because they played with a different 'gang,' I hardly saw her. I had only just started my apprenticeship as a Fitter and Turner at the Small Arms Factory, so I sort of knew Robert because he was a second year apprentice in the same factory. I find it strange that although we lived quite close we rarely mixed; we seemed to play with those in the same street and treated the others as outsiders.

The Jones family were outsiders; I remember this name because I had heard this poem.

> "Here lies the body of Herman Jones,
> Underneath these polished stones.
> His name was Brown Instead of Jones,
> But Brown won't rhyme with polished stones."

Mr Jones was a light skinned aborigine, and worked in an office somewhere in town, and as far as I knew, didn't drink with the miners, and seemed to live a fairly private life with his family. Mrs Jones was to me even then, stunning, although slight of build she was very well proportioned, and had the shiniest black hair which fell in loose curls over her slender shoulders, Ellie, probably three years younger than me was going to turn out the image of her mother with the same black hair and those beautiful wide eyes peculiar to these indigenous people. Robert was very much like his father, slight of stature thin legs common in aboriginal people, and light skinned. As far as I knew they were quite intelligent and well mannered, always doing well at school, and a few years later, Robert became top apprentice of the year.

Rita had her arm around a sobbing Ellie as she guided her into our kitchen, in those days the kitchen was the main room of the house, all activities were carried on in the kitchen, probably because the fireplace was there and I suppose the radio, no TV in those days. Rita sat Ellie down by the fire and mum was fussing around making a cup of tea for us all, a cup of tea was mums' way of settling everyone down, whenever there was a problem to be sorted out mum would say, "Let's have a cup of tea and think about this."

The story finally came out that Ellie had been teased and bullied at school and Rita had stepped in to protect her. My heart went out to both of them in that moment, I felt like hugging them, but wasn't sure if that would be appropriate.

Over time, I got to know Ellie well, and through Rita, began to get an insight into how difficult it is for an aboriginal family to fit into a white society. I would hear stories of how that black bastard (Mr Jones) would bash his wife and that he wouldn't give her enough money to buy food, they would back this up with, "Look how skinny they are," apparently ignorant to the fact that as aborigines they were a perfect size and weight. We knew that none of these accusations were true, and we probably knew them better than most. Mrs Jones had become one of mum's best friends, but dad didn't mix with Mr Jones, which was probably because Mr Jones didn't drink or gamble.

I asked dad one day why people didn't like Mr Jones and dad explained it with "Not all people dislike him, I don't for instance. Mr Jones is very protective of his family and has probably stood on a few toes, he managed to get Robert an apprenticeship where a lot of white people missed out, they have to blame someone for their failures, and because the Joneses are different they are easier to blame, I know that I had a bit of trouble when I got you in as an apprentice over some of the others." "Some of the kids call Robert yellafella, where does that come from?" I thought I might as well find out as much as I could about this confusing subject. "It's not a nice term, but it means half cast, the ones who don't like Mr Jones call him that too." Dad could see my confusion and patted my arm saying "Don't worry about it now, just make sure you don't go along with any of this, take people as you find them, and not how others might say they are, you know what's right, listen to your gut instinct." That advice has held me in good stead for many years.

I always thought the Joneses had more money than us, as they had nice furniture and Robert and Ellie were always clean and neatly dressed, not that we weren't, but I think mum let Rita and I get away with a fair bit as far as tidiness went.

The shit, so to speak, hit the fan when, after a particularly bad bullying Ellie attempted suicide, again everyone blamed Mr Jones, but we knew that he had nothing to do with what was wrong with Ellie. Thank God we had mum, she was strong and full of unconditional love and explained to us how fear makes good people act in cruel ways. We had no fear of the Jones family and loved them as our own, so we had a lot of trouble understanding the hatred shown towards them because they were black.

Dad was transferred to another mine near Newcastle and we lost touch with the Jones family, now fifty five years later, that first introduction to what can only be called racism is still strong in my mind.

However racism is not all about colour as I have come to learn through my life's journey. There is something strange in the Australian culture; we don't seem to take well to foreigners. The English were called ten pound poms, because they paid the fare of ten pounds for the boat trip from England to Australia. The Italians were called; Spags or spaghetti eaters, the Japanese, Nips, and the Chinese were called chinks, there were many more. There was a saying that foreigners came here to marry our prostitutes and bring them down to their own level, maybe we have improved, at least I hope we have. I realise also that many of our judgements were based on fear. As Australians, we had it pretty good, and we had fought hard to get our lifestyle, so we were very protective of it, I know that I went through the process of disliking foreigners because they worked too hard, and thought that it wouldn't be long before I would have to work as hard as them or become unemployed. Maybe it is the same with black or indigenous peoples; maybe we are afraid that if we stop holding them down and keeping them in their place they may take over. Isn't fear the reason that we don't want them to have land rights?

I don't know if that's true or not, but it is human nature to protect what we have no matter by what means we get it. I'm not saying it is right, but it is as it is.

We seem to conveniently forget that our grandparents came to Australia under similar circumstances, and now that we have a foot hold, don't like others to come and share our wealth, it's not surprising then to see why the original inhabitants are acting in much the same way. I can't find any evidence as to us being invited here.

It may seem as I'm judging here, but I'm really stating facts as I see them. From a spiritual point of view, I don't see how anyone can lay claim to that which is God, for God is all nature, men and land alike, we are one, and as such all must walk free without fear.

I had just finished my apprenticeship and was having a working holiday in New Zealand, it was quite a culture shock and everything seemed to be about five years behind Australia. There seemed to be a good relationship between the Maoris and whites, but what I noticed more than anything else was the police. Dressed in their button up uniforms and 'Bobbie' helmets, they would walk the streets side by side smiling and greeting the passersby, and no guns were evident, I know it has changed quite a lot since then, I was there in 1963.

As a white man working, and living with indigenous people, I feel very privileged to have had the support that I have received. This became evident the very first time I worked with them. I had had enough of city life and headed west from Brisbane where I got a job ring barking trees, the idea being to kill the trees so that grass could grow for the sheep to feed on.

Before I continue I would like to take you back to the beginning, the full story needs to be told here.

Any mention of AA is only my opinion and experience, and is not AA approved, nor necessarily what AA agrees with.

This is a story which leads into the darkest depths of hell and insanity, and out the other side to a wonderful life, completely free from the past, to an enlightenment few get to experience, it is a journey, which is not really a journey but a gradual awakening, as to how the God of my understanding has been with me throughout. When I use the word God, it is a simplification of what I call the Higher power, or Higher self, and is not necessarily meant to signify a religious God. God to me is not a being but a state of being, and that state of being is love. So love has become my religion.

What I have today is not a new life built on the old, but a completely new life, living each day as it is. The old becomes nothing more than the wisdom learned from experience.

I have opened my heart and feel that I have left nothing of importance out; many names outside of the family have been changed to protect their anonymity, and I have kept the wording as simple as possible avoiding the use of flowery words. If anyone wants to share this or any part of it, please feel free to do so.

"When the heart listens, Love will be heard.'
Ronald Russell

Chapter One

Last drink... August 8th 1984

How did I get here, feeling cold and damp, I think the bloke next to me shit himself, or is it me? I don't know any more, it doesn't matter, got me goom 'Metho' and port wine to keep me warm, must be a dozen under this bridge tonight, the Salvos couldn't fit us in, cops just drove past, shined their torch and drove on, must have a full house as well,...Poor bastard over there spewing his guts up, I don't spew no more, just stay drunk. I like it when they dry me out in the hospital; they give us a bath, and a bed and good food. Last time I got three weeks, it was real good, they gave me something to stop the D T's and friggen night mares, works as good as the grog. The nurses are real nice; they smile and wipe the sweat off your forehead, makes you feel loved, its nice being looked after, don't get looked after much, don't remember getting loved much since I left mum. Had a missus and a couple a kids but they left me, or maybe I left them, doesn't matter either. Doctor reckons me livers shot, wants me to quit drinking but I feel ok after me three weeks in hospital, maybe I'll slow down a bit...

Maybe the doc was right. Lotta pain in the guts, they called an ambulance again, I'll probably be ok in a week or two, like, I always come good... What am I doing here, poor bastard over there spewing, feel like I've been here before, but I'll be ok, me mates getting a couple a flagons tomorrow, he'll probably get a bottle a goom to make it go further...

I'm in the ambulance again... How did I get here?....

This is not where this journey ends, or where it begins, to find the beginning we must go back forty years to a small country town in New South Wales, Australia.

"Am I mad in a world that is sane, or sane in a world that is mad?"

I find it strange how some of our earliest memories stay with us throughout life, through all our depressions, those dark times where all memory seems lost, and then through the highs when everything is forgotten in the excitement of the moment.

One of these memories is from when I was three years old and my new baby sister Rita was being bathed on the kitchen table.

We had and old galvanised tin bath about 18 inches deep and 3 feet in diameter. I remember I couldn't see properly, so one of my aunties picked me up for a better view, I can clearly see mum cradling Rita in her gentle hands, I always saw mum with gentle hands. Thinking about it now, everything about mum seemed gentle, of average height and weight, with light brown hair, I suppose she was the image of the average mum, but to me, especially in later years mum was the only definition I had of love. I can see her now, kneeling in front of me on a winter's morning, warming her gentle hands by the fire, and then massaging the rheumatism out of my painful legs. Sometimes, if mum needed to discipline me she would chase me around the block with a stick, much to the delight of the neighbours who cheered us on. This one time, I was too fast for her and by the time I had reached the second corner knew that she couldn't catch me, she was nowhere in sight. Thinking she had gone home I strolled the rest of the way home assuming that whatever she was after me for would be forgotten. "I'm too fast; she won't be able to catch me again." My mind was elsewhere as I rounded the large shed which stood on the last corner.

"Ahh Haa. Got you, thought you were too smart for me." My heart was in my mouth, the surprise almost floored me, so unexpected. Mum had me in a bear hug, laughing and kissing my cheek, her problem apparently forgotten in the exhilaration she was feeling in surprising me. This was my mum, she had my heart, and I never wanted to be bad again, surprising how quickly we forget, isn't it.

Lithgow, where we lived, was a coal mining town about one hundred miles west of Sydney, I remember it being very cold in winter and the smoky railway shunting yards welcomed the travellers leaving the lush greenery of the mountains before beginning the steep decent down the winding road we called the forty bends. Even though the town was growing toward being a city, it was still small enough for everyone to know who everyone else was, and, unlike many cities today, the whole neighbourhood consisted of people who were actually neighbours.

The Roberson's lived next door, Mister and misses Rob; Mr. Rob had a jersey cow and walked up to the paddock every morning to milk it. One morning while I was playing out the front, Mr Rob, who was quite tall and walked with a slight stoop to his shoulders, called to me as he left his front gate, 'Want to come and milk the cow this morning, your mum said its ok?" I was off like a shot. Mr Rob handed me the bucket and I instantly became an important part of our community, not that I knew what community was, I was only six at the time, but I knew that none of my friends had milked a cow. "ere, fill this bag with some of that chaff," Mr rob was pointing to a large steel bin filled with chaff and Lucerne hay. We had just entered an old run down shed made from corrugated iron, inside was a very fat jersey coloured cow, already standing at the bail waiting for its morning feed "This is Jessie, by the way, Jessie the Jersey," Mr Rob laughed at his own wit. Well, I had seen plenty of cows before, but never up close, there seemed to be an enormous energy emanating from such a large animal, and I wasn't too sure I wanted to be this close. Carefully keeping my distance, I emptied the chaff into the feed bin while Mr Rob put Jessie into the stall; Jessie's hind leg was tied back and she was chewing happily while Mr Rob milked her. I was fascinated by the stream of pure white milk forcefully entering the bucket each time the teat was pulled. "'Ere, come, you can 'ave a go if you want." Mr Rob didn't pronounce his H'es. "Whoa not behind there, might get kicked," I jumped quickly back; pretty sure I didn't want to get kicked. Mr Rob pulled me close to him and placed my hand on the teat along with his.

There is something very intimate about touching a cow; I suppose touching any animal in what I feel may be a sensitive area. I was in absolute awe as my hand closed around the soft, warm teat and the milk started flowing as my hand worked under the guidance of Mr Robs' firm hand. "Your turn, just keep doing it the same way." I kept going in what I thought was exactly the same movement as Mr Rob, but the flow of milk stopped. "Ere, try again," he said as he placed his hand alongside mine. This time I was able to keep the flow going, I was thinking, "I can milk a cow," but at the same time, thinking, "I'm never doing this without an adult". You know, I've never lost that fear of large animals, I absolutely love riding horses, but I'm always aware of their raw strength, and their ability to use their own mind if they so desire.

Dad was a coal miner, and as I was growing up, I have the memory of dad leaving for work with his tin lunch box strapped across his fairly broad shoulders, dad was around six feet tall and with his solid build, black curly hair, and ready smile, one would call him handsome, and despite his many failings, I'm pretty sure mum loved him.

Friday was dads' payday, I can see Rita, mum and myself, all sitting in the kitchen singing what I then thought was mums favourite song.

"Clap hands for daddy coming down the wagon way,
Clap hands for daddy coming down the wagon way;
Clap hands for daddy, 'cause he's coming home to mummy,
Clap hands for daddy, he's got a pocket full of money;
Clap hands for daddy coming down the wagon way."

Dad rarely came home on a Friday afternoon; it must have been heartbreaking for mum. I didn't know it then, but dad was a heavy drinker and gambler, and as I grew up I realised that there never was enough money. It must have been hard for dad bringing up a family in the depression, especially being a drinker and gambler, oh yes, I know we can say he had a choice, but I'm not too sure of that, some of dads' friends ended their lives during these difficult times. Dad had told me stories of work mates cutting fingers off to get the compensation money.

It wasn't all doom and gloom with dad, he never punished me, he left that up to mum. I have a few memories of travelling in the country in dads 1928 Ute, picking up fallen trees for fire wood, that was a lot of fun, we were all together on those occasions. Quite often during weekends, to make ends meet, dad would pack the ute with swags and prospecting gear and the two of us would spend the weekend prospecting for gold. Dad taught me how to divine with a green forked branch cut from one of the many willow trees growing along the creeks. I was to use this skill later in life to divine for water. We would build a wooden frame beside the creek with a slide a little like a slippery dip, a blanket was laid on the slide and then 1x1x12 inch pieces of wood would be nailed across this blanket at about 10 inch intervals, this was called a sluice box, the idea being to put the box into the running creek and then shovel the sandy sediment we collected from the river bed onto the slide, the running water would wash the rubbish away and leave the heavier material trapped in the 1 inch cross timbers, this was then collected an washed again in our gold pan where the gold was separated from the other lighter material.

Then there were the rabbits. When I was about ten, dad would take me shooting rabbits, I became a very good shot, each rabbit had to be shot in the head, no holes in the skin or flesh, the meat and skins were sold to the local butcher. There wasn't much waste in those days, we found many ways to make ends meet and the wolf from the door, old newspapers would be collected and sold to the butcher or the fish and chip shop as wrapping paper, kids could be seen collecting drink bottles at footy games and other events and the deposit money claimed, and in the season whole families were out picking the juicy Blackberries from their thorny vines, what we didn't use ourselves were sold to the local shop and then sold on to the jam factories. School holidays would see me and a couple of mates digging potatoes on a farm belonging to one of dads' friends. I remember mum wanting to go to work but dad wouldn't allow it, he was adamant that a woman's' place was at home with her children; I think it was more about pride and him being the provider for the family, or, maybe if mum was at work he might have had to spend more time at home.

We always played outside when it was fine, I was probably around six years old when I took my three year old sister to the creek for a swim. We had removed our clothes when our neighbour, Mrs. Livingstone, we called her 'Dead brick' spotted us and reported us to mum. I got a good hiding when mum got us home, I remember thinking it was terribly unfair because I couldn't see what we had done wrong. Today I realise that it was swimming in the unsafe creek, rather than nude bathing that had mum worried.

The kitchen was the centre of activities in our home, that's where the fireplace was, next to the fireplace in its own alcove was the old cast iron slow combustion stove, these were surrounded by a brick wall which was the back wall of the kitchen. Above the fireplace ran a mantle shelf where mum had placed many of her treasures. I can still see a picture of Jesus on the cross, glued to a piece of cardboard; underneath were the words "Not my will but thine be done" "Forgive them for they know not what they do,"

In those younger years, up to the age of about ten, I don't remember seeing dad around the house very much; it was as though there were only three in the family, although I did see him every morning when he left for work at the mine. We were only one hundred miles from the ocean but I didn't get to see it until I was ten.

Rita was always in the back ground in those early days at home, she probably had other special times with mum. Mum and I would sit by the fire and have many philosophical talks, probably from the age of seven or eight. A lot of our talks were about mums ideas of religion. She told me that the Old Testament talked about fear and punishment and she didn't believe in the devil. Mum followed what Jesus taught, and she explained that he was only human like us, and that we were all children of God, but he believed in God more than we did, that's why he could heal people, mum told me she could talk to Jesus. I didn't understand how this could be until I was nine or ten years old.

The coal mine where dad worked was not far from our place, about one and a half miles, a railway line ran from the main line to the "pit" which is what we called the mine. It was a Sunday, no trains were supposed to be running, so my friends and I were playing on the railway bridge that crossed the creek about a mile from home. We weren't allowed to play on the line, but we were kids and it was Sunday. The top of the bridge was 60 to 80 feet above the stony creek which trickled its way through the valley. My friends had climbed down under the bridge and I was in the middle, probably one hundred feet from each end. I glanced up to see mum running flat out waving her arms, hair blowing wildly as she ran, I knew I was in trouble, and I prepared myself for a tongue lashing. The look on mums face as she got closer frightened me, maybe it was fear that I saw, I'm not sure, all I remember is mum dragging me off the bridge in the direction she had come, she seemed to have amazing strength as she supported me while dragging me off the bridge and over the embankment. Up until that moment I hadn't heard a sound; We came to a stop less than six feet below the line and as I looked up I saw and heard the terrifying sight of a large steam train passing directly above our heads, it seemed to be all noise and moving pistons and things, with white hot steam hissing loudly from the safety valves. Then just as suddenly it was gone, disappearing in the distance around the curve and through the cutting, making its way innocently towards the mine where a load of carriages awaited its arrival. Everything was silent. We didn't hear a whistle so we don't believe the driver even saw us. The train had come around a blind bend which ended just before the bridge; it would have been difficult for the driver to see us.

It was a quiet walk back home; we were both in shock I suppose, but later with a cup of tea in hand, sitting at our usual place beside the fire. I asked mum, who had been unusually quiet, how she knew that I was in trouble. Mum glanced up at the picture of Jesus glued to cardboard on the mantel piece and in an unusually solemn tone said, "I don't know, I honestly don't know. I was just sitting here thinking about nothing in particular, when a voice, which wasn't a voice, maybe a feeling, told me to get to the railway bridge as quickly as possible, I had no idea why. It was as though I was controlled; I just ran as fast as I could, I had no idea you were on that bridge." Mum was silent for a while, "It wasn't me that pulled us off that bridge; it seemed to be just happening." After a long silence, I feel we both felt that somehow, Jesus had taken control of that situation. From that day on, I knew there was, and at times experienced, a power greater than myself at work in my life.

Mum and I had many fire side conversations over the years, and looking back, I believe mum had a similar understanding of a higher power as I have now. That is, that we are all one in the harmony of love.

Inspirations

There is no danger or hurt in love, only peace. I understand we all have our Journey, and each life is unfolding as it is, We are all at the right place in this moment, and are experiencing exactly what we are meant to experience, good, bad, or indifferent, and each experience will bring wisdom, for wisdom is experience learned. I'm just happy to be experiencing this with my fellow travellers, knowing that no one is further ahead, because there is no further ahead, there just is, and we are...

Living in love with you eternally.

Ronald Russell   Namaste'

Chapter Two

Meanwhile life went on, dad continued to drink and gamble, he trained greyhound dogs for racing and it was often my job to put bets on with the starting price bookie across the road; I got a few bob from his winnings and much to mums disgust he allowed me to have a small bet for myself. "Great addictions have small beginnings." In adult life I became addicted to gambling as well as alcohol, drugs, and tobacco. That's not for now. For now, I believe I had a wonderful childhood, playing outside until the evening meal, and then again under the street light until we were called in for bed.

We had the radio but no TV in those days, I loved to get up early in the morning, go into the kitchen and listen to the cowboy singers, Slim Dusty, along with Smoky Dawson and Gene Autry were among my favourites. I loved poetry, Henry Lawson, Banjo Patterson and Henry Wadsworth Longfellow. Mum used to read to Rita and me, sometimes she would read some of her own poems, they often made me sad. A little like the song "Old Shep", it is the story of the friendship between a man and his faithful dog Shep. Shep had reached the end of his life journey and the man had to put him down by shooting him. I loved the song but I cried every time I heard it. What is it that keeps us listening to stuff that makes us cry, maybe it's like an addiction, where we think, we'll be able to handle it this time, only to go through the same experience once more.

Playing again on that same railway bridge, almost one year later, this time on the girders which were part of the frame work; Robert my friend who lived two doors down was 'Tight rope' walking across a beam, a distance of about twenty feet; He was half way across when he noticed a Tiger snake curled up on the other side, as he tried to turn around he slipped and fell the sixty or so feet to the stony creek below. We hurriedly climbed back down the embankment to Robert who was laying with his body on the stones and his head just in the water which was already turning pink from the bleeding cut on his head, as I pulled him from the water one of the boys ran for help; The ambulance had a difficult job getting him safely up the steep embankment but they managed with our help.

Robert came home from hospital blind, although only temporary and with a fractured skull, and collarbone. He couldn't read, so I would take my poetry books down and read to him, I would read comic books and try and describe the pictures as I read.

Another activity we loved was to climb the mountain up to the cliffs on top. About half way up the cliffs, a ledge ran horizontally across the front, probably eighty feet above the base. It was fairly easy to climb up through crevasses in the cliff. We would have competitions rolling the large rocks off the cliff and down the mountain.

Henry was battling with this extra large rock which was partly buried, we could see him straining, trying to pull the rock free when it suddenly let go, it rolled over the edge taking Henry with it. I heard the rock hit the bottom and a split second later Henry landed. I remember the sickening feeling I had in my stomach, this couldn't be good. Henrys head had hit a large boulder and was smashed in on one side; it looked like his brains were all over the rock. I felt sick to the stomach we could see he was dead, I had never seen a dead person before, skin all splotchy pinks, greys and whites. While writing this I'm experiencing that same feeling of dread and fear.

Before leaving this era, I would like to relate a terrifying experience of my own; I had built a canoe by folding a piece of corrugated iron in half, the ends were nailed together through a piece of board and other boards kept the sides apart. I had taken it up the creek to the swimming hole to try it out; I found that I couldn't climb into the canoe while it was in the water so I pulled it onto the bank and sliding my legs under the board holding the sides apart, pushed with my arms until the boat slid down the bank into the water. I was alone and was thinking how everyone would want to ride in my canoe, I was really proud of my idea. As the canoe entered the water at an angle, the front, instead of rising went straight under the water and kept going under as if it was a submarine. I was panicking, with the water up to my shoulders and the canoe still sliding deeper down the bank, I tried to free my legs but they were stuck beneath the cross boards. I realised the more I struggled to free my legs the deeper the canoe entered the water. I was screaming for help by now and the water had reached to just below my mouth. Everything seemed to settle in that spot, I realised that I could still breathe as long as I held my head back and stayed still. It was getting late in the afternoon, you've no idea of the fear I was feeling, or the terrifying thoughts that were going through my head. I kept calling out for help but I was sure I was going to die, "What happens if it rains?" I answered myself. "The creek will rise and I'll drown for sure." My neck was already getting tired and I'm imagining, slowly having to drink water instead of breathing. 'Bang,' a gunshot, 'bang,' another, I started screaming at the top of my voice, but the excitement made the canoe sink a little further into the water. I could barely keep my mouth above the water. I screamed again, and again, I'm thinking they must hear me.

It must have been five minutes later, when Mr Williams came into view above the embankment. "What are you doing in there he asked while hurriedly climbing down the bank. "I could hear someone calling out but couldn't see anyone." After sliding the canoe into shallow water, he helped me out then pulled the canoe up onto dry ground. I was sure I was going to get into trouble, but instead he rolled the canoe over and stood on it with his large boots and as it started to crush under his weight, he casually stated "Better get rid of this, don't want to be fishing anyone else out of the creek tonight, lucky I was out this way after rabbits this afternoon, I was going to go up stream, but I had a feeling to come this way." Mr Williams, who was a rather large man, around thirty years old, with a reddish complexion topped with fiery red hair, put his arm around my shoulder. "Scary isn't it? I had a similar experience when I was about your age, I thought that I was gone then, but for some reason I'm here for you today," I never mentioned this at home and I don't think Mr Williams did either. All food for thought isn't it. The train line was a major land mark around our home. It was the dividing line between the town and the bush. If one crossed the line and walked east, he would end up in danger of being lost among the mountains and valleys which made up the Blue Mountains. Many have met their demise in those mountains. Snakes were always a problem because of the proximity of the mountain and the creek, especially Tiger snakes, they were very quick and very deadly, there were a few Red Bellied Blacks but they were much slower, we just took them in our stride. We had an outside 'Dunny" or toilet and one morning mum found a large brown snake coiled up beside the pan and dad had to shoot it.

I can still see the Dunny man carrying the full pan on his shoulder out to the horse and cart which followed him along his rounds, his head and shoulders covered with a waterproof cloak to keep the spills from the overfull pans from touching his body. There was a joke getting around about the Dunny man. He and his offsider were just finishing their last run before lunch, so they pulled the horse and cart up under a shady tree. They were seated on a seat which straddled the poo in the tray of the cart. Dan 'The dunny man' was passing a slice of bread and butter across to his mate when it dropped right into the poo, in a flash Dan had picked it up, and while passing it on again to his mate said with a smile "Bloody lucky that time, it landed butter side up."

One of our jobs was to take a bucket up to the line and collect the coal which had fallen off the overflowing coal carriages; we needed this coal for the fire at home, sometimes we would throw stones from the top of the cutting and knock the coal off the full carriage. Quite often, the workers, who travelled on the back of the coal carriages would push extra coal off so we could collect it, there was a lot of good will like that around in those hard times.

School was a bit of a pain, I was bullied quite a lot, and to make matters worse the miners went on strike for quite a long time. This was the depression time, not much food or money, and now dad wasn't working. The school gave all of the miners' children hot soup and a bread roll to help feed us. I don't know what it is about kids, but the worse off you are the more you get bullied. At the other end of the scale those who were very intelligent copped it as well. Some slightly older boys caught me behind the toilet block one day, they were smoking, "Hey sissy, come here and have a smoke." I'd had trouble with these boys before, and I was really frightened. "I don't smoke," I replied. "You dobbed us into the teacher didn't you." Before I could deny this, three of the boys had me by the arms and were dragging me into the toilet block, I was struggling but they were too strong. "Stick his head in the toilet." I was crying as they forced my head down into the toilet bowl. "Now flush it." I can't remember ever experiencing so much fear. I couldn't escape they were too strong, I could feel the water in my ears and because my head was upside down it was running up my nose, I felt that I would drown. I was saved by the teacher, Mr. Brown; I felt the pressure release from my arms and neck and pulled my head up just in time to see two of the boys go flying across the room. He was ropeable; his face was bright red with anger as he ordered the boys to his office. He checked to see if I was all right and I assured him that I was. In reality I was far from all right but I'd had enough, I just wanted to get out of there.

Something happened to me that day, something changed inside of me. For the first time I really knew anger. Although being rather thin I was wiry and very fit, quite tall with very long arms; Most of my clothes were either too big in the body or too short in the sleeves. Within a week I was in trouble with the boys again, there were two brothers, one my age, Robbie Harris, and the other, Alex, one year older, he was the best fighter in the school. I was running after a ball on the bitumen play ground when Robbie, tripped me. I went flying, skidding on my hands and knees, taking skin off wherever I touched the ground. As I felt the pain, something strange seemed to happen, I wasn't really aware of what was happening, I could see myself as from outside myself. I had got to my feet and was punching Robbie Harris, he fell to the ground and I kept on punching, other boys were trying to pull me away but all of those years of being bullied, and especially the toilet incident, were finally finding release. A few days later, Robbie's brother Alex picked a fight with me because I bashed his brother. I was really scared; his friends were with him, I knew there was no backing down, by now a dozen or so boys had gathered around. I tried to explain that it was Robbie's fault that we fought, but he just pushed me and threw a punch. Again, I don't know, I stood looking down at him lying on the ground with a bleeding nose, I don't remember hitting him. His friends wanted to take up the fight but the other boys stepped in. That was the last fight I had for many years, I realised that I could handle myself in rough situations but I was scared of myself, worried that I might go too far. This fear has arisen many times over the years and now sixty years later I'm still aware of it, but no longer afraid of myself.

Inspirations

The most important thing to remember is, it doesn't happen all at once, everything is broken up into a moment, which is why we need a direction, so that each moment builds onto the one before. We have to remember this and practise it daily. Grab this moment of excitement and carry it onto the next, and the next and the next. ~ Always remember, each moment spent dwelling on your past, is a moment lost, and may even change your direction, that's what living in love means, it means you are one with the creator, and as such are a creator yourself. Imagine what a mess you would create if you kept changing directions while creating your world. So my friend, Live in Love, and create your world, you are not separate, you are one with this universal Love.

Living in Love with you eternally.

Ronald Russell   Namaste'

Chapter Three

I'm fourteen and a half years old and the high school intermediate certificate was coming up, this is the exam I have to pass if I'm to be accepted as an apprentice Fitter and Turner at the Small Arms Factory. Mum and dad had arranged through friends to have me taken on as an apprentice in the New Year. It wasn't easy to get an apprenticeship in Lithgow, so mum was on my back to pass my exam. I'm not the brightest of scholars, just achieving a pass at the best of times. To make matters worse, I had missed a lot of schooling through illness and the extra study was taking its toll on my health.

There wasn't much time for play these days. School, then study, then study again at weekends, I seemed to be always tired.

It was Saturday morning, I had slept in, and I could hear the family in the kitchen having breakfast, feeling grateful they hadn't wakened me, I washed my face, and was drying off when I noticed my eye looked exceptionally large, another inspection revealed that it wasn't my eye that was large, my whole face on the left side had dropped, it looked hideous, I tried to form my mouth into a whistle but my mouth pulled across to the right side into a sneer, The left side of my mouth drooped down so much that I needed a piece of wire hooked into the corner of my mouth and looped around my ear to keep it up, my left eye wouldn't close and the skin around it drooped down so far that I could see the raw flesh below the eye. I had no idea what was happening, maybe I'm dying, I was really frightened, the more I tried to make it work the worse it seemed, nothing on the left side of my face worked. I tried to smile and all I achieved was that terrible sneer. I was calling mum. "Mum, Mum, My face isn't working", all the while trying to put it back in place with my hands. The fear in my voice had mum beside me in moments, closely followed by dad and Rita, "What is it, what's wrong?" Mum was gently removing my hands away from my face. The look of horror on their faces didn't do much toward making me feel any better. "Is it painful, can you feel anything, can you feel my fingers?" Mum was touching my face with her fingers. "No, yes, I mean it's not painful, yes I can feel your fingers." We were all at a complete loss as what to do. I could see that mum was trying to be strong, she held me and led me gently into the kitchen, at the same time motioning to dad to get Mrs Rob to come from next door. Mrs Rob, one of the few people in the street who owned a phone called an ambulance and mum and I were whisked off to hospital.

They say what doesn't kill you makes you stronger. I definitely wasn't too sure about that while waiting in the outpatient emergency ward, and glancing across at my mother's distressed features, I would bet that she wasn't too sure either. The doctors and staff in the emergency room, were at a loss as to what the problem was, they were all fairly young, The senior doctor was called and after a short examination diagnosed my condition to be Bell's Palsy, a condition where a nerve in one side of the face is damaged and as a result the muscles in that side don't work, and without muscles to hold everything in place it drops. I had a million questions but mum was voicing them. "How did it happen, can it be cured, and how long will it last?" The doctor quieted mum with a hand over hers. "There's not a lot we know about it, but it usually disappears in about three days. However if it hasn't healed in six weeks there's a chance that it won't." "Isn't there anything we can do?" Mum was still understandably worried. "Well, we'll wait for the three days, then if there is no improvement we can arrange physiotherapy, it consists of light electric shocks being delivered to the area around the nerve, hopefully stimulating it to working condition, we can also work out a set of facial exercises, they may help strengthen the left side muscles." The doctor was writing on a pad. "In the meantime we can get a support, a hook to hold your mouth up in place and well arrange for an eye patch." The doctor was standing, helping mum to her feet. "That will be ready tomorrow if you can drop by and pick it up, come back in a week and we'll see how it is going."

The next day we picked up the patch and hook for my mouth, but by the end of a week there was no improvement with my face. I started facial exercises in front of a mirror, trying to get the left side working. I slowly discovered that if I didn't smile so hard, my mouth wouldn't pull into such a sneer. Once while practising, Rita made a funny remark about the exercises. Without thinking I smiled at her while watching myself in the mirror, a genuine smile, yes my mouth still pulled to the side, but unlike the practise smiles, I noticed that my eyes were smiling. This was a big break through, although it has taken many years to accept that, although I can't smile with my mouth, people don't really notice, a genuine smile comes from the heart and radiates through the eyes. You may have guessed by these last remarks that the nerves never recovered, but after three or four years of practise I was able to close my eye, my mouth stopped drooping but still pulled to one side, especially if I was tired, and later on if I had been drinking.

My self esteem suffered greatly, mainly because I felt that I couldn't smile properly, and that others might not see my eyes smiling. We take so much for granted, we don't realise how important a small thing like a smile is. Life must go on; I passed my exams, and started my apprenticeship. I was earning three pound six, about $8.00 per week; I think the adult pay was about $40. I was still only fourteen years old and I wouldn't turn fifteen until the first of April, Yes, I'm an April fool baby, mum used to tell me that because I was born on April fool's day, others couldn't play the tricks on me, I quite liked that idea.

I honestly don't know, maybe I'm a mummy's boy, but the second and third year apprentices decided I had to be initiated, four of them caught me in the toilet and took my pants down, then they got some Prussian blue, a blue greasy substance used in the trade for marking; They proceeded to smear it all over my genitals, I was really embarrassed but guessed this happened to all new apprentices, it took about three days to clean it off, I was thinking that it's worth it, at least now I'm accepted, or that's what I thought. All went well for a few months, then one day during lunch, some of my first year mates realised that I didn't swear, they tried to make me say the word shit, but I wouldn't, they stripped my shorts off and threw them up on the roof and wouldn't allow me to get them until I swore. After a while, I was thinking that I've no choice, so I said it, the word sounded so strange coming from my mouth, so I said it again, and it wasn't long before much worse swear words were sliding easily off my tongue.

I was the youngest among my class of apprentices, and towards the end of the second year a few of the boys were becoming sexually active. I had a few girlfriends who I took to the church dances and they seemed to like me enough to come to the pictures with me, but as far as sex went, it had to wait until after marriage, or at least that's what I believed until one of them fell pregnant.

One of my friends was telling me about his sexual exploits, and I asked him what it felt like, he smiled, probably embarrassed, I pushed him for an answer, "Come on, I won't tell anyone, what does it feel like? He really was embarrassed, "Come on, what's it feel like?" "It doesn't feel like anything, I dunno, I suppose it's like putting it into warm tea leaves," He turned and walked away. No prize for guessing what I tried when I got home.

Bill Haley came to Lithgow in the film "Rock Around The Clock," it was showing in the theatre for a whole week, I went every night, those a little older were rocking and rolling in the isle, I was hooked, I started to go to Saturday night dances, something I really loved to do, dancing was a way of escaping through movement, especially rock and roll. I was terribly shy around girls and had a lot of trouble asking girls to dance, at this stage I was very aware of my inability to smile openly and what I called my crooked face. It's strange how we judge ourselves much harder than anyone else does. I can't recall anyone ever mentioning what I might call my disability. At least not until my first defacto relationship many years later when my partner called me "crooked face white trash," in a drunken argument.

I had been practising rock and roll dancing at home with Rita; we would go out on the lawn with our record player blasting away and dance for hours. Every movement from the film would get a try out, some we would master, others were a dismal failure. The lawn was the best place, because I insisted on throwing Rita over my shoulder, sliding her between my legs rolling her over my back, and pulling off some pretty mean swings. To her credit Rita was an excellent partner, and because of our very close relationship, although hesitatingly at first, trusted me not to hurt her. Of course there were a few accidents but Rita was pretty tough having grown up playing with mostly boys, as play mates.

I was almost seventeen, and the dance had been going for an hour or so, I had already danced a couple of old time dances with my church girl friends but every time I asked the rock and roll girls I got a knock back. The dance hall was a basket ball court in real life, with its polished wooden floor, and benches around the sides. As was the custom in those days, the girls would sit along one side of the hall and the boys on the other. To ask for a dance I had to walk across the hall in full view of everyone, and to me every one was watching and waiting to see what the outcome would be, the trouble was, I knew the outcome, it happened every time. That long, lonely walk across was nothing to the walk of shame on the way back, 'If only the floor boards would open up and swallow me." Mum used to say to anyone who would listen, "My Ronnie's a good boy." But as far as I was concerned good boys didn't get bad girls. It was after one of these knock backs, that I had walked outside of the hall, dejected as ever, when four motor cycles roared into the no standing zone in front of the hall, no helmets in those days, but short leather coats, wide belt buckled with a large polished brass buckle at the front, neatly pressed jeans and highly polished pointy toed boots. They were one or two years older than me. The Fonz, yes that would be the easiest way to describe them, and no sooner had they had arrived than half a dozen pony tailed girls with short, short skirts were climbing all over them. Everyone was joking and laughing as they headed around the back of the hall, arm in arm, a couple of the bikers with two girls. To me, these were the bad boys, these were the girls I wanted, the ones brave enough to buck convention. I actually saw one boy get put into the back seat of a police car, only to quickly slide across and escape out the other side door, my heroes. I was left standing alone in the cool night air, then just before they went out of sight around the corner, Jacko, who lived close to me and was a miner with dad, called out, "Hey Ronnie, want a drink?" beckoning me with his free arm, in the hand, a bottle in a brown paper bag. Wow! They recognised me, I'd never drank alcohol before, but if these boys had asked me to jump off the Sydney harbour bridge naked, I would have done so. After ten minutes or so and a few swigs from the bottle of Green Ginger wine, everyone decided to head inside, Jacko had loosened my tie, and told me to undo my coat, a final check and Jacko was satisfied, we headed into the hall, me, feeling pretty important and light on my feet.

Marjory was an older sister of one of my friends, two years older than me, quite well proportioned, and wearing flat shoes and bobby socks, topped off with a flared skirt that swung out revealing dark blue panties as she twirled around, the perfect rock and roll outfit.

Because of my friendship with her brother, we became close friends. She was an excellent dancer and because I knew her, I asked her for a 'Jive,' our term for rock and roll. Everyone seemed to be watching, I felt as one with Marjory on the floor, no more timid Ron, alcohol had freed me, most of the night was spent jiving with Marjory, but two other girls beat her to the dance by actually asking me first. Instantly, I had become the best rock and roll dancer in Lithgow, at least in my mind. I never went to another dance sober.

Just as an aside, Jacko was to teach me a life lesson a couple of years later. Jacko was on the same bus as me, he was carrying a one year old baby. The bus was fairly full and a middle aged woman entered the bus, even though Jacko was holding a child, and still dressed in his bikie outfit, he gave the lady his seat, then, as he alighted first, he paused to offer his free hand to another lady leaving the bus. I heard a little later that he had a nice home, wife and two lovely children. 'It doesn't matter what clothes we wear, or how we comb our hair, it's the heart we live through that makes us what we are.'

After work the bus would drop us at the top end of town opposite the Court House hotel. My mate Tony and I would drink four pints of beer between five and six before the pub closed for an hour, presumably to allow drinkers time to go home and eat dinner. We would then walk the mile home singing at the top of our voices. It has always amazed me how; good singers seem to be able to remember the words of heaps of songs, but those without a good voice like me, have trouble remembering the chorus. By the time we were home we felt sober, I don't think mum realised I had been drinking, but I always felt terribly guilty seeing that I had promised her all those years ago that I would never drink and end up like dad. I had started smoking as well, but I could easily justify it in those early days, "I'm only smoking three a day, I'm only smoking five a day, Gees, get off my back, I only smoke a small packet a day," and so it goes.

I bought my first car, with dads help. A 1936 Chevrolet convertible, with a dicky seat in the back. I painted it fire engine red, and purchased white walled tyres. I'm still a virgin, at seventeen, but I'm hoping this car is going to change all that. Tony was the expert; he had already slept with a girl. Seven o'clock in the evening sees us driving down the main street, hood down, dicky seat up with a few drinks in side us and a bottle of Barossa Pearl sitting beside us on the seat, Tony calls it leg opener, Tony is leaning out of the car trying to chat the girls up, I'm driving, cigarette in my mouth, arm over the side door, trying to look cool. No luck, oh, we picked a couple of girls up, but the Barossa Pearl never worked. A couple of weeks later we decided to drive to Katoomba in the Blue Mountains, Roger, a work mate lived there, so we picked him up and three girls he knew, we drove to a lookout overlooking the Three Sisters, a famous rock formation in the area. These girls were out for fun, by this time we each had a girl, Kate, my girl, and I took a blanket from the dicky seat, and headed across to a reasonably private area hidden from the others. This was all very embarrassing for me, lucky I had a few beers on board. Roger had told Kate that I was a virgin, so Kate was all for being my first. Kate was very good looking, a blond pony tail set off what I would have to call a cheeky smile, a short skirt, and flat shoes, my ideal girl. I was a bit clumsy at first, but Kate guided me expertly. We stayed on that blanket for hours, I had fallen in love. I won't say any more about that night, except to say that it felt nothing like the tea leaves my friend from years before had described. Kate and I formed a steady relationship, and I would drive down there every other night for the pictures or a dance. Kate left for Europe with her parents eight months later, I was devastated, we kept in touch for a while, and then the communication gradually stopped.

I was playing darts now, and every night after dinner I would drive into the local to play, I discovered that I was very good at darts as long as I had just the right amount of grog in me. I would say to myself "The trick is to control how much I drink", but how to do this? I tried all ways, like drinking light beer, or eating a large meal before drinking so it would absorb the alcohol and release it slowly; another trick was to drink a lot of milk in order to put a lining on my stomach, nothing seemed to work. I thought that I could just slow down, I was thirsty. Ah, ha, that was it; I seemed to be thirstier than other drinkers, so I would drink lemon squash or some other non-alcoholic drink. The final solution, although not perfect seemed to be a late start, if I came to the pub later, I would still be in good condition to play, but that didn't help my condition at the end of the night. Mum was becoming a problem too, she was getting on my back about drinking, and I was starting to have some serious arguments with her which left me feeling lousy. It all came to a head one morning, I had just driven back from Katoomba after a big night out, I reckon that I drive better with a few in me, and mom met me at the door, boy was she angry, she wouldn't let me in the house, she screamed. "If you want to live your life as a drunk, you can go to work as one." "I'm still in my suit," I replied lamely. "Go in your suit, let everyone see you as you really are, go on get out," with that she threw a tin of condensed milk at me, I caught it and before I knew it I had thrown it back at her and hit her on the temple, while writing this the fear is rising up in me, even after all these years. Mum dropped to the ground, hands clutching at her head. I didn't know what had happened at first, it was an automatic reflex, I found myself holding mum in my arms, blood running from her forehead, my heart beating so, so, fast. Mum, my mum, what have I done? She was crying, I was crying. "Better go to work son, I'll be all right." "Are you sure?" I just wanted to stay and hold her. "Yes, go to work, we'll talk later." I'm having a lot of trouble staying balanced writing this; I didn't expect that I would relive the scene, my heart is thumping. If only it could have ended there, I love my mum so much.

I went to work in my suit, everyone had a go at me, best thing they had seen in ages, but I wasn't laughing, I couldn't wait to get home to mum. "Straight home today," I told Tony, "going to have a spell from the grog for a while." Mum was waiting as I walked in the kitchen, a look of; I'm not sure, maybe apprehension on her face. She allowed me to hug her and tell her how sorry I was. "I know she said softly I know you love me, but we need to talk". It seemed that she was soothing me, instead of the other way around. "I'm sorry about this morning, I was terribly, I mean I am terribly frightened about what is happening to you, I see your father coming out in you, drinking every day, I was very angry, I'm sorry I threw the tin at you, I just don't know what to do." "I'm sorry too mum, I've decided to stop drinking, I told Tony on the way home." We hugged, it was over for now.

Instead of drinking, gambling became my new obsession, I had always played the horses and dogs, but now, instead of going out at night to the pub, I would go to the two up game which, although illegal was held just behind the police station. Two up was commonly known as the 'Swy' game. A Swy was four shillings, and that was the minimum bet allowed. Many a time did I go to the game with four shillings and leave with hundreds of pounds, only to give it all back the next night. Two up started during the Second World War, and was played by the ANZACS, it was tolerated by the law on Anzac day, but local police turn a blind eye to it at other times as well, for reasons we won't go into here.

Two pennies are placed tail up on a small flat board called a Kip, The person throwing the coins in the air, called a' Spinner' would try to get the coins to land with two heads showing, if this happened he would get another turn. The ring within which he stood to throw the coins consisted of a piece of tarpaulin about ten feet square, surrounded by wooden bench seats on which the gamblers sat. Each gambler would get a turn to spin the coins for a minimum bet of four shillings, but they could bet as much as they wanted as long as there was enough money around the ring to cover his bet. I remember one night sitting with my legs apart, with money piled between my legs as high as my knees, there must have been thousands of pounds there, enough to buy a house. The trouble with gambling like this, money means nothing, it's coming and going all the time. I left the game owing my mate five pound that night. Yes, I was temporarily upset, and called myself a mug, but I was back for more the next night, after all, I really only lost the five pound I borrowed plus the five I started with. Such is a gamblers life.

My apprenticeship was almost finished, and a few apprentices had found an advertisement in a Sydney news paper. A new paper mill was being built in a place called kawerau in New Zealand, all types of tradesman were required, fares paid over, and then back at the completion of the job, full accommodation and keep also supplied. I talked to mum about going over there, she wasn't too happy at first, but gave in after a while; anyway we didn't have the job yet. Two weeks later we were told we were off to N Z in a month, as soon as our apprenticeship was finished.

Inspirations

HOME----To enter this place of trust, this place where I see the utter uselessness of control. To see the whole picture, but only work on part of it. To see life and death as one. To realise that I am always doing my best with what I have in this moment. To realise I will do what I will do and nothing will alter that. To realise nothing I do or will do, is neither good nor bad, it just is. To realise that each past experience has brought me to this moment now, To understand that I can't strive for love and trust, but can allow them to enter my life. To realise that in this moment, I am exactly where I'm supposed to be, and everything is as it is. To realise that when I'm afraid I'm afraid and that's O k too. To know the everything and nothingness of love, and that wisdom is experience learned. When I know all this....I am home.

Living in Love with you eternally.

Ronald Russell.   Namaste'

Chapter Four

We arrived in January; I was still nineteen years old. We didn't see much of the New Zealand city life; as we were whisked off to the paper mill, as soon as we arrived. Our housing consisted of hundreds of separate huts, called Dongas, about eight feet wide and ten feet long. I was given a job as an instrument fitter, I'd never heard of one, so had no idea what one did. It wasn't long before I was fitting the copper tubing to instruments throughout the mill with the ease of the instructors who were teaching us. I had started drinking again, but not too heavily, I was there to save money, although there was a few times when I didn't make it back to work after a counter lunch in the pub, anyway, I reasoned, I only drink beer, unlike some of my friends who almost always drank spirits.

Roger, My friend from Katoomba, had come over with us and he decided to buy a Norton Motor bike. We were earning good money, with nothing to spend it on other than a few beers here and there. I decided to buy one too, mine was a Triumph Thunderbird. I had my licence from Lithgow where I owned a bike for a few months. The bikes opened that part of the country up to us, we travelled to Rotorua, and visited the Maori villages, saw the lava pools and breathed the horrible stench of the sulpha steam that escaped from the storm water drains in the town, and we visited the amazing glow worm caves, where thousands of tiny glow worms would light up a great cavernous area. Winter time would see us riding to the snow fields for ski-ing trips.

We didn't need bikes for this next almost unbelievable adventure. Opposite the paper mill stood Mt Edgemont, quite high with miles of rolling foot hills leading up to it. Five of us decided to hike up to the base of the mountain with a packed lunch and a water bottle each. We estimated it would take about three hours each way so we left at eight in the morning, we were following a long narrow path, probably made by sheep. The country side changed into areas of rocky outcrops. It was while passing one of these outcrops that Normie, a slightly built quiet chap who didn't drink, noticed the opening to a cave. "Let's go inside" I was all for exploring it. I was already down to the floor of the cave about six feet below; the opening was big enough to shed light into the cave. I stood and looked around, there were shelves carved into the side of the cave, one about one foot from the ground another about four feet above this. On these ledges were bodies wrapped in rotting cloth, some in canvas breaking up with age, they weren't actually bodies, but skeletons, some were partly clothed, one had a three cornered hat on its head, similar to those worn by sea captains a couple of hundred years ago. There were three caves like this, some of the skeletons had been disturbed, and only a skull and a couple of bones remained. I was all for taking a skull back to camp and putting a light inside it, thankfully, the others were horrified at this idea, reminding me that this was probably a Maori burial ground. I had little sleep that night, dreaming of headless bodies walking single file down the long winding path towards our camp, thank goodness I never took that skull. We never went back, but we enquired about the caves from a couple of Maoris who worked with us. They knew nothing of the area because they were not local, but reminded us that it would definitely be sacred ground and as such we were to stay away. I still wonder why it was not marked and protected, as it was probably over one hundred years old, and I wonder also, if it is still there today.

After nine months at the mill, Neil, another Aussie, who was fairly new to the job and I decided it was time to move on and see the south island of NZ. I had been gambling a lot on a game called Heads and

Tails, a dice game similar to two up, so I didn't have a great deal of money. He had a bike also, so we rode our bikes to Wellington where we decided to stay for a while and get a job. The cheap boarding house we stayed in had eight other boarders; I suppose you could call them no hopers, of varying ages from between thirty and sixty. I had never been exposed to this side of life; this was my first boarding house, but by no means the last or worst. That first breakfast should have been a warning signal as to where I was headed. Neil and I shared a room, and were told that breakfast would be at seven the next morning. As Neil and I walked in to breakfast, we were greeted by a few grunts from one or two of the men seated around the table, over on a side table stood two toasters and a couple of opened packets of white bread. We followed the example of the others, as no one seemed to care enough to show us the ropes. While we were toasting our slices of bread, the hostess came in with a large glass bowl full of steaming hot frankfurts and placed them in the middle of the table, the bowl was heaped so I just continued on buttering my toast. As I turned to walk to the table, I stopped dead, the bowl was empty, I couldn't believe it. I looked at Neil and he just shrugged his shoulders as if to say, "Buggered if I know". I wasn't too worried, I had just come from a camp where they were always re-filling the bowls, I placed my plate on the table and went back to the side table and made myself a cup of tea. Neil and I sat at the table, nibbling at our toast and sipping our tea waiting for the next bowl of frankfurts. The other guests were leaving the table; I glanced across at Neil again only to be rewarded by another shrug. We were just finishing off, everyone had left, and the hostess, Mrs Jones came in to clean up, a slightly overweight motherly woman. "Morning boys, did you enjoy your breakfast?" she had a genuine smile of affection on her face. I felt comfortable enough to tell her that we didn't get any frankfurts and that they were all gone before we got to the table. "oh, I'm really sorry, we allow for three each, some only eat two, so there's usually enough to go around." "They were gone before we got to the table." I could hear myself whinging now. She ignored my whinging tone. "I see you boys aren't used to this lifestyle, some of these blokes are really greedy, and don't care for anyone but themselves. They probably just stuck the frankfurts in their pocket to eat later." Neil was shocked. "Without any wrapping?" Mrs Jones nodded "It's how it is with these people. She had finished cleaning up. "We'll I'd better get this lot cleaned up." She gave us a dismissive smile as she left for the kitchen. We weren't backward in coming forward for breakfast again. Neil got a job in a factory, and I got a truck licence and got a job driving a brick truck. Although it was very hard, I really enjoyed the outside work. I was building up my arm and shoulder muscles as well.

Six weeks later it was time to leave Wellington for the South Island, first stop, Christchurch. We sold our bikes, as we decided that a cheap car would be more comfortable, and we could sleep in it, instead of paying board. It was night time and the weather was very rough when we boarded the ferry which sailed between Wellington and Littleton on the south Island. I was terrified that the ship would roll over, it certainly felt like it would, we couldn't see out and we weren't allowed on deck. After the first hour I became violently ill with sea sickness and I still had the whole night to go, death would have been easier I thought.

Christchurch, the Garden city, the city of bridges and bikes. A beautiful, flat, crisp clean city built on the Avon River. We stayed here long enough to buy a 1931 Essex car for ninety pound, side running boards and all. The pins that held the back of the front seat in an upright position could be removed and the seat fell back forming a double bed.

Loaded with tinned supplies, a frying pan, a billy, tea and sugar, and a loaf of bread, we were off to tour the South Island. First major stop was Invercargill where we found work in a meat works. While in Invercargill, we drove down to the Bluff, the bottom, or southern most point of New Zealand. It didn't get dark at all; the night stayed a sort of twilight until the sun came up next morning. Two weeks pulling sweet breads, 'a gland in a sheep's neck' was enough for us. We headed up the west coast to Milford sound, a beautiful bay surrounded on three sides by magnificent cliffs. Trouble struck just as we started on the steep incline down the winding road leading to the bay. There was a loud grinding noise coming from the engine followed by billowing clouds of steam. Neil was driving and he had the presence of mind to turn the ignition off, stopping the engine from turning and doing more damage. The engine cooling fan had come lose and made a hole in the radiator the size of a fist, the radiator was boiling because most of the water had escaped. We were stuck at the top of this very steep descent. What to do? As we saw it, we could wait for another vehicle to arrange a tow truck, or we could attempt the dangerous descent without an engine, we chose the latter, and with the car in gear and the clutch being used to help the brakes we made the hair raising trip to the bottom. To my surprise, the problem was fixed with two tins of bars leaks.

Christmas day saw us leaving the beautiful serene snow covered view of Mount Cook mirrored in the wonderful blue of Lake Pukaki. Neil was driving again, a quiet country drive, when we came across half a dozen geese, there didn't seem to be anyone around so we decided that we had stumbled on Christmas dinner. I was standing on the running board while Neil chased them in the car. After a few attempts I managed to grab one by the neck, it almost jerked my arm out of its socket, it was so heavy. A farm house suddenly came into view and the goose was squawking for its life. I had managed to climb back into the car by this stage and was trying to ring the goose's neck to keep it quiet, it wouldn't stop. "For Christ sake shut the bloody thing up." Neil was driving like a madman trying to put as much distance as possible between us and the farm house. No one heard us, we drove on another ten or so miles to a bridge, a crystal clear stony creek bubbled its way down from the snow covered mountains to this bridge. "Now for Christmas dinner," Neil pulled the car under the bridge; I was still fighting the goose, so Neil retrieved a knife from the glove box and cut its throat. It wasn't too long before we had a fire going and the gutted goose was cooking on the fire, feathers and all. We had the billy on and it wasn't long before we were eating the toughest goose in history and loving it. "Merry Christmas" we clinked our tea mugs together. Life is wonderful.

Back in Littleton, we had sold the car for five pound more than we paid for it, and Neil has flown back to Australia. I'm working in an engineering workshop performing maintenance on the merchant ships in port. I would love to go back to Australia by sea. The sea has always called to me. I loved travelling across to Manly on the ferry, the smell of sea water and oil, the thump of the engine as it fights to turn the prop in its endless revolutions through the water. I know that I get sea sick but I'm sure that I would overcome that in time. I'm living in one of the hotels in Littleton so I'm drinking quite heavily, there's another pub just down the road where the seamen drink, I'm spending a lot of time with them lately, talking a lot about getting back to Australia by sea. Without a seaman's ticket or being a registered engineer it doesn't look possible.

A new ship has just come into port, general cargo, heading back to Sydney as soon as it unloads; it's the weekend so I'm spending a lot of time in the bottom pub with the crew. There's talk about a way that I can get back to Australia with them. It wouldn't be legal but they are telling me that they do it all the time. One of the mess men is going to introduce me to the steward who will hide me until we get to sea; he has his own quarters so I will be able to stay there unseen for the trip. I'm really excited, so I'm spending a lot of time with the steward, he seems like a really nice person, very kind, and generous with his shouts. It's three in the afternoon and we are to sail first thing in the morning. My bags are packed, and I've given notice at the hotel.

I found my boss from the maintenance workshop in the top hotel and told him that I wouldn't be back on Monday. Over a beer he questioned me as to how I got to go on the ship, he had been good to me and I trusted him so I told him that I was stowing away with the chief steward. He looked a little concerned, "They didn't mention the term 'ring bolt' did they?" I was surprised that he knew. "Yes as a matter of fact they did, it's a seaman's term for stow away, isn't it?" The boss, whose name is John put his hand on my shoulder, "Don't get on that ship, you're in big trouble if you do." "I'm not worried". I answered back, a little annoyed that he wasn't happy for me. "The steward will be looking after me." "Oh, he'll be looking after you alright, when you get to sea, you have no choice other than to do what the steward and his mess men want." He paused for effect, or maybe he just wanted to think about his words, then, his mind made up he just came out with it. "Ring bolt means that the steward and possibly his mess man will be putting their bolt in your ring," "F*ck me," I blurted out in shock as I realised how close I had come to being on that ship, and of the consequences involved. "Yes, f*ck you," John smiled, "and you wouldn't be the first, that ship has a bad name." Oh well, looks like I'm flying home, feeling lucky.

Inspirations

CREATION.....In the beginning, Nothing Else existed in the vast nothingness we sometimes call Infinity. Nothing Else wished there was Somewhere Else, and as soon as Nothing Else thought about Somewhere Else, Somewhere Else became real, and Nothing Else realised that there had always been Somewhere Else, but it didn't exist until thought created it. Now, realising that thought was the creating energy, and being pleased with Somewhere Else, Nothing Else wondered if there was Something Else, and behold there was Something Else. Things were going great for Nothing Else, having created Somewhere Else and Something Else, Nothing Else wondered if there was Anything Else, but when Anything Else was observed, Nothing else discovered that there was Nowhere Else, and it was then that Nothing Else realised that Somewhere Else, Something Else, Anything Else, and Nowhere Else, all existed, and came from the same vast infinity, because there is nothing else.

Living in Love with you eternally.

Ronald Russell.   Namaste'

Chapter Five

Toukley is a small holiday village south of Newcastle. Dad has transferred to a coal mine in this area. Rita is working and living in Newcastle. Mum and dad, have no children now to look after, and are enjoying the warmer climate, they offered me a room in their new project home, on the lake, dad is fishing a lot instead of drinking and they seem happy. Why not stay for a while? I know mum would like that, and I sense that dad would like to bond as well. I managed to get a job building wheat silos at a factory about ten miles away and bought a motor bike to get to work. I stayed three wonderful months, I even had a steady girl friend, and then I got itchy feet, and wanted to move on. I sold my bike and moved to Sydney, where I got a job with a labour hire firm. This was really the perfect job for me. When factories would shut down for maintenance the powers to be would contact my boss and order labour. I was on call with a dozen other tradesmen of different trades. If they wanted a plumber there would be one or two plumbers on the job and the rest of us would say we were plumbers, and so it went with whatever tradesmen the hiring firm required. I earned big money when I worked, being paid double time most of the time. The trouble with the job was the time off between jobs, I would spend this drinking in the hotels while playing darts or pool, after a while I started missing work, and it wasn't long before I felt the axe about to fall. This became a way of life for quite a few years, I would work a few months, the first one or two very hard to prove myself, then the pressure would get to me, and I would come unstuck with the grog, and then move on just before the axe fell, I had no trouble getting jobs, and doing them better than most, I just couldn't keep up the pace.

I was talking to a cab driver who owned his own cab, and he said that he would give me a job driving for him if I got my licence. A month later I was cruising around Sydney looking for fares. There isn't a lot of money driving cabs, but you can supplement it with tips and multiple hiring, which was not allowed but everyone did it. I was cruising in Redfern one night at around 2 am when out of the corner of my eye I caught a glimpse of an arm waving, I pulled over closer and a girl of about seventeen ran to my cab, I had to look twice, she didn't have a stitch of clothing on, she was crying and told me she had no money, she asked if I could I take her to the police station, which I did after retrieving a throw rug from the boot to cover her nakedness and hopefully make her feel a little more comfortable.

We had a special call sign for the radio if the driver is in trouble with a passenger. It made me feel much safer when I witnessed it being activated. The call went out from a cab about one minute away from my position, I immediately headed there and to my surprise there were three cabs there already, the aggressor had ran off but the driver was safe.

I had a close shave one night; I picked up a fare wanting to go to Camden, in those days an out of the way new suburb with a lot of bushland. At night, passengers usually get into the passenger's seat next to the driver, this chap, about twenty five and quite large, got into the back, Then he slid across until he was sitting behind me, my intuition went into over drive, the hairs on the back of my neck were standing up, I knew that I could be in trouble, but I couldn't call it in because I was only going on instinct. We hardly see another passenger along that road at night, it's just not a place that's safe to walk, but as I rounded a corner, partly out on the road, was a man dressed in overalls flagging me down. "Don't stop," the chap behind me was saying, and by rights I wasn't supposed to. But there was no way I was going to Camden alone with this bloke in the back.

"I'm going to I replied," more firmly than I meant to. "There won't be anyone along here for ages." I had already pulled up, and the new comer was getting in the back. "Thank god you turned up, I'm broken down about a mile back, and no way of letting my wife know, I've Just come off shift. He was going to a street very close to the first bloke. "You can drop this new guy off first, if you want, I'm in no hurry" I was having no part of that. "No, she'll be right, you were first, and he only lives another minute away."

After I had dropped them off, I felt exhausted, the strain was incredible, I realised that I had hardly been breathing; I pulled over at a street light and took a few breaths. For some reason I decided to check out the back seat. As I opened the door, there on the floor right behind the driver's seat was a skinning knife about eight inches long, he must have dropped it when I picked the second fare up. Intuition is an amazing thing. I handed the knife in to the police with a description of the offender, only to find out that no one of that description lived at the address I had given.

The best rank was at Kings Cross, where I became a favourite with the girls of the night, gays and the Jewel Box crowd. The Jewel Box was a night club where bi- sexual and cross dressers would perform, I was always friendly and always gave them good service. I always smiled to myself when a gay guy got into the cab, they would slide across the front bench seat which was designed for three, then place their bag, which most of them carried, on the outside next to the door, some would even say jokingly, "Now this is nice and cosy," I didn't mind, we knew each other, I had made my sexual preferences clear, and we trusted each other.

It was the same with the prostitutes; I never went with them, although I did try once or twice. Prostitution was a business, to be kept separate from personal life, and so was cab driving. That didn't mean that I couldn't share a unit with them, which is exactly what I did. There was a big new block of about fifty units that had just been built overlooking Tamarama beach, the rent was too high for my two lady friends so we decided that we would share four ways. My friend Shawn, Lindy and Margie, all agreed on the condition that we would remain only as friends and not form a relationship with each other. Shawn worked as a barman in the Bondi Hotel just down the road. Next door lived four of the Jewel box crew, they had heaps of parties, to which we were always invited, but they weren't our style. Although it was interesting sometimes, to watch the boys pashing on out on their balcony overlooking the ocean, pink and purple hair, all thrown in.

It was at this beach, one morning, that I experienced another unexplainable phenomenon. It was summer, and as was my habit, I would go to the beach straight after my shift of driving ended. It was around five in the morning, the sun had just poked its head above the far horizon, sun beams glittering on the wave tops like fairy jewels, not a cloud to be seen and what breeze there was stirred the sea just enough to create more wavelets for the fairies to place their jewels upon.

No one was on the beach at this time as it was a sheltered beach. I was swimming close to shore because I'm not a strong swimmer, I became aware I was too far out; I could feel that familiar knot starting to form deep in the base of my stomach, that feeling that's saying "Hey something's wrong here, I'm losing control." I could feel my heart beating faster. I panicked and started to swim towards the shore getting further away every moment. I doubled my effort, feeling my stomach begin to knot up even more with fear, I just kept swimming, nothing seemed clear to me anymore, I was swimming over arm, but I was six feet under the water, I was trying to reach the surface that I could see above, I have no idea how long since I had taken a breath, I can't remember being out of breath, I just remember feeling very tired, I couldn't move my leaden arms any longer, the surface seemed further away, it doesn't matter anymore, I know in my inner most being that I have nothing left. Thoughts are entering my head, soft and lulling. 'You're feeling really tired, it's too hard, it would be nice to just have a sleep, rest now, close your eyes and rest,' A voice, maybe mine, I don't know, the last thing I remember was the peace I felt as I closed my eyes. I awoke high and dry on the beach, there were a few people around by then, but with the position I woke up in, it probably looked as if I was just sleeping on the beach, as far as I know no one knew what had happened. How did I get from under the water and travel at least one hundred yards to shore and wake up high and dry? Today I know.

'There are no mistakes in Gods world.'

A few weeks after this experience I had a minor accident in the cab, I ran into the rear of another car and the older woman passenger complained of whip lash, I had been drinking as usual and her husband accused me of being drunk. 'Drunk' the justifications started in my mind. 'Drunk, they don't know what drunk is, I never get drunk while I'm driving, the last beer I had was two hours ago, and anyway I had a good feed afterwards. Shit, it wasn't even my fault, that silly bastard in front stopped for no friggen reason whatever, it could have been a lot worse if I hadn't been on the ball, that old bitch hasn't got whip lash, they just want to use me for their insurance.' They were all for calling the police but as they got out and onto the footpath I took off. I knew that I would be in serious trouble, so I parked my cab back at its garage, phoned the owner to say I was sick, and keeping the takings, walked a block and caught another company cab to the unit, where I packed my gear and left, leaving a note saying that I had family troubles and that I was sorry for letting them down, and that I wouldn't be back. I felt I owed them that much, they had been good friends. I was on a train to Brisbane within the hour.

I never heard any more about the incident in Sydney, but I wasn't taking any risks. I got a Queensland licence, by transferring my NZ licence across, and for many years I was worried about the NSW police catching up with me.

Inspirations

For too long I allowed the world to make me hard. I grew an impenetrable shell that nothing from outside could penetrate. I had become small and bitter, then in a moment of weakness I allowed someone to hug me lovingly. That was enough, somehow that love penetrated the hardened exterior and began to grow from within. Today I know, this love became one with the love that was already within. As this love grew the walls softened and crumbled, and the fear that built them is no more. Now the strangest thing is happening, Love hasn't stopped expanding, and is becoming one with all Love, and there is no need for walls.

Living in Love with you eternally.

Ronald Russell   Namaste'

Chapter Six

I had a yearning to go out bush, out west among the trees and wild life, cities were not for me. I worked at the Littleton oil refinery for two months as a pipe fitter and welder until I had enough money to head west. I bought an old 1956 FE Holden station wagon and headed off to who knows what.

The small western town I arrived in was typical of most western towns in Queensland, and depending on their size, had one or two hotels. It was Friday afternoon, and two, four wheel drive Utes were parked out the front of the only hotel. Around the side in the shade stood two horses tied to a rail leisurely munching at, what was probably judging by their interest, some luxury food in feed bags fixed around their necks. Pubs are the information centre of the bush, you can find out who died, who has just had a baby, who is sleeping with whom, and where the work is. I was interested in the work.

As a white man working, and living with indigenous people, I feel very privileged to have had the support that I have received. This became evident the very first time I worked with them. I had had enough of city life and headed west from Brisbane where I got a job ring barking trees, the idea being to kill the trees so that grass could grow for the sheep to feed on.

In the Buddhist tradition there is the term 'Ignorance', it means doing things we aren't aware of and thereby creating suffering within ourselves. I find it a little sad that in many instances the very people whose life and culture depend upon the preservation of the environment, especially in the outback areas were employed to destroy that very environment, and often for not much more than rice, flour, tea and tobacco.

Upon my return from NZ, it was in this destructive environment that I innocently found myself. I, and I'm sure my aboriginal work mates weren't aware of the damage the removal of trees would do to the environment, the money was there so maybe we didn't want to know, I only know it was a job, the money was good and it was in the fresh outback air, I wasn't prepared to think about much more than that.

If you are going to look for work you have to look like a worker, and you have to fit into the environment. Before coming out west, I visited a Salvation Army opportunity shop, where I purchased Jeans, boots, an R M Williams body shirt, and even though I don't like wearing hats, I was lucky enough to find a well worn Stetson. "Clothes maketh the man." That's bull shit, but they create a good first impression, after that it's up to the man.

I entered through the front door, and as my eyes adjusted to the darker light, I could see two men playing pool, they stopped to observe me as I walked over to the front of the 'u' shaped bar, they were dressed in clothes almost identical to the ones I was wearing, I had chosen well, I reasoned that these were the owners of the horses out front, because the other two occupants were wearing greasy overalls, 'probably the local mechanics,' I thought. The barman wandered over, and raised his eyebrows in question as to what I was drinking. "Schooner please," I replied to his un-worded question. He returned with the beer. "Travelling?" he asked. "Yeah, but looking for work as well, anything around?" The barman shrugged, "Bad time, shearing's finished, Collin might know," he looked over at the two men by the pool table. "Hey Col, fella wants ta know, any work about?" Col put out a work hardened hand. "Col Green." I took his hand in a firm shake. "Ron Russell" He was studying me closely "Shearing's f*cked, whater ya do?" "Bit a anything," I copied his way of speaking, "Just come up from the wheat 'round Griffith," I lied. I didn't want to let on I had mechanical experience either; I wanted to work outside, not in some workshop. "It's the end a the month, Scotty'l be in the sarvo, ya eva used 'n axe?" "Not much, but I reckon I kud learn, can I get you an ya mate a beer," I asked pointing at his empty pot. It's a good way to become accepted in a new town. The barman bought over two pots and we walked over to the pool table. "Ken, this is Ron, lookin for work, told him 'bout Scotties team, what d ya reckon?" Ken took my hand. "Yeah maybe, he's always lookin for some silly bugger who'll work for 'im," Ken was smiling. You could see they were mates with Scottie.

Following in dad's footsteps, I had become quite a heavy drinker and gambler, and this is what I was doing in the only hotel in town. The Saturday afternoon horse races were on the radio and there was an illegal starting price bookie in a small room out the back. Although being illegal these bookies were tolerated by the local police, probably because there was no other way to place a bet other than travel a long distance to a race track. I enjoyed a game of darts and pool, and was quite good at both; these were my excuses to be in a hotel. My biggest problem was that once I started drinking I got the taste and found it very difficult to stop, so I had to be very careful, especially in a new town where I was trying to make an impression.

It was while I was playing darts that a truck loaded with eight men pulled into the pub, six aborigines and one white bloke jumped off the back, and the truck took off again, probably to the driver's home.

I watched as the white bloke walked to the bar and bought six cartons of beer, and then one by one he carried them outside to the waiting aborigines who took off in the direction of the river. I struck up a conversation with the white bloke and found it very interesting that he was the only white bloke on the back of the truck. He was of a wiry build with snowy white hair, probably a couple of inches shorter than my six foot one inches. What struck me most was the bluest of blue eyes which shone beneath a furrowed brow that bush men get after years of peering over long distances in bright sunlight. He wore the traditional dress a bush man wears when going to town, complete with his Slim Dusty hat and boots. Slim Dusty was a Country and Western singer, very popular in the bush in those days, and whenever there's a do on, someone will have a guitar and be singing Slim Dusty songs. Anyway I get to talking to this bloke who tells me his name is Sandy, due to the white hair. What I forgot to mention was the fact that he had the traditional wide nose of an aborigine. Maybe I was staring, I'm not sure but he noticed me looking and smiled showing perfectly even white teeth and told me that two of the boys outside were his half brothers. I couldn't believe it, how could someone with snow white hair and blue eyes be aboriginal?

It turns out that Sandy's father was a Swedish seaman, who came to Lightening Ridge, and like many others in those days, planned to make his fortune mining for opals, while there, he shacked up with Sandy's mum and had two children, Sandy and Leah. The fortune didn't eventuate and he went back to sea, leaving Sandy's mum no option but to go back to the river camp and her family, where they still live today.

Sandy invited me to join him back at the camp, so we got a carton of grog each and headed down to the river. The camp consisted of about ten corrugated iron shanties, spaced about twenty yards apart, just upstream from the road bridge.

I was feeling pretty uncomfortable being introduced to Sandy's family, lucky I had a few drinks under the belt; they gave me a little Dutch courage. I was welcomed with open arms, and made to feel comfortable, actually, I felt like I was being welcomed into the family, which was a new feeling for me, especially since I had only just met this wonderful family. Maybe they could see goodness in me that I was afraid to recognise in myself.

We cracked the beer open and handed the bottles around. I noticed a few older males "Grey Beards" around the shanties but they seemed content to sit cross legged outside their doorway, keeping their own counsel. Sandy's mom wouldn't have been much over forty, she had long shiny black hair, slightly curled which flowed gently over her slender shoulders. I had an instant liking toward her, almost as if we had met before. I was reminded of Mrs Jones and Ellie, and wondered if they had ever lived on a river bank.

Sandy's mum, I never got to know her name, I just called her Mum like everyone else, anyway, she made us a wonderful dinner, which I found out later was Emu meat, made into a wonderful casserole served with rice and damper, a cup of tea was served from the billy beside the camp fire, then we all got stuck into damper and treacle, for sweets. Today you would pay thousands for this experience. It's amazing what we take for granted in life isn't it?

Later we went outside, and by a large camp fire sang Slim Dusty songs to a guitar played very professionally by Sandy's younger brother.

We all had a great night and mum made up a bed for me on the ground, the mattress was made from woven Pandanus leaves with the prickly bits stripped away. A grey army blanket served as a cover, it was summer so the blanket was plenty of cover on the warm night.

The grog and I never mix well and it was no different this night. Around about three in the morning, I awoke to the pleasant feeling of someone lying beside me in a spooning position, my head was still a bit groggy and it took a while to realise that Sandy's sister Leah had climbed in to my bed, and as she cuddled up to me I realised she was without clothes, my head cleared miraculously and every part of me jumped to attention.

I was a lonely twenty three year old male and had enough booze in me to throw caution to the wind. We made love that night, although quietly, and the fear of being discovered certainly heightened the thrill of the experience. I have many failings and one is that I fall in love easily, and now I was in love with Leah.

Leah's eyes were the roundest dark pools that seemed to swallow me as I looked deeply into them, she was Mrs Jones, Ellie and her mum all rolled into one, Ahhh, Leah.

The next day we rested, and I was introduced to the neighbours and made feel very welcome. In the daylight I got my first glimpse of the camp in its entirety. The houses were all built in a similar fashion, with a sturdy frame built from timber cut direct from the surrounding bush, with corrugated iron walls, and roof which sloped backward from the front. Lined along the whole back of the shack were about eight, forty gallon drums, ready to catch the rain water from the roof. This was used for drinking and cooking. River water, carried from the river in five gallon drums was used for everything else. One thing I noticed was the way the floors were made, they were made of trampled earth and kept spotless with constant sweeping, and all in all I found their homes to be spotless throughout.

On Sunday evening the truck pulled up to the camp, as the driver climbed from the cab I saw that he was a tall, red haired, red bearded fellow who wore a checked shirt, open at the front revealing a broad chest covered in tight red curly hair. He looked more like a lumberjack than a cowboy; even down to the boots which were the conventional style without the high heels like the cowboy boots.

I was to find out later that he had spent most of his life wielding an axe of some sort or another. He had a slight Scottish accent and his voice, although gentle carried a confidence seen only in men who really know who they are.

Sandy was speaking to him and I noticed that every now and again they would look my way. Shortly, Sandy made his way over to where I was standing; he looked excited as he proceeded to tell me what had transpired between him and the driver. It turns out that this was the boss, and Sandy had just asked him to take me on as a ring barker, promising to look after me until I got the hang of it, grabbing me by the hand he excitedly dragged me over to the boss, "Scotty this is my friend Ron, he's the fella I was talking about." Scotty took my extended hand in a firm shake, the kind of a hand shake that tells you that there is a lot of power there but the owner doesn't have to prove anything. "Sandy here tells me you're looking for a job, ever used an axe before?" I let go of his hand "No, not a lot, but I'm a quick learner and I'm not frightened of work." Scotty was checking me out, then with a shrug put his hand out again, and as I took it in mine he said, "Sandy reckons you're ok and that's good enough for me, be here at five in the morning, we've got an hour travelling to the camp, Sandy 'll tell you what you need." We finished the shake and he turned to climb into the truck, "No grog, It's a dry camp." I smiled to myself; I'm more than happy with that, it'll give me a chance to dry out and save some cash.

We arrived at the camp about six thirty next morning, on the drive out I noticed the wildlife along the way, Kangaroos and Emus lined the sides of the road, or I should say track, it was hardly wide enough for the truck to navigate, around one bend was the biggest eagle I have ever seen, we disturbed it eating the remains of a lamb that it must have caught a little earlier, as it took flight I could hear the noise of its massive wings as they grabbed hurriedly for air on its upwards flight, I would estimate the wing span to be well over six feet possibly seven. I loved the open spaces of the country, I was happy; this is where I belonged, the simple life. I loved the idea of working in the bush, and getting paid good money. Today I realise that you can't put an old head on young shoulders, we had no idea of the damage we were doing to the environment.

The camp kitchen was already set up; it consisted basically of a large canvas tarpaulin stretched over a pole which was held up in the forks of two trees and pegged down at the sides. Under the tarp was a long table with a dozen chairs down the sides. Just outside of this tarpaulin, and under another was the cook's four wheel drive, with the back full of all kinds of cooking gear, some I'd never seen before.

The cook "Cookie" was a black fella, probably around sixty years old, large torso, topped by the most open, smiling, grey bearded face I have ever seen, his eyes under that bushman's furrowed brow were bright, and the only words I can find would be to say that they were full of mischief. As it turned out "Cookie" had led a very interesting and colourful life and rarely took life too seriously.

I had an instant liking toward him and soon realised that I wasn't alone in that. Cookie greeted everyone with that wonderful smile topped with a handshake or hug. The say an army runs on its stomach, well it's no different with bush workers, Cookie could make a banquet out of bacon, beans and damper, oh, and flies. The flies were so bad, I've never seen flies like it, we would try and eat damper and jam at smoko with our cuppa, but the flies would cover the jam in moments and then get stuck, after a while we turned a blind eye to the flies and ate whatever was on the damper.

Everyone had their swags, I was given mine, and it was basically a canvas sleeping bag with a hood for the wet weather. After a wonderful breakfast of lamb chops bacon and eggs with fried tomato and toast, everyone prepared for work. The boss, Scotty called me over to the truck, and from behind the seat produced a brand new axe, the head was smaller than the axe I used to cut firewood with at home, not much more than half the size, but bigger than a tommyhawk. "Break it you pay for it" He was smiling as he called Cookie over. "Cookie, I'll get you to look after Ron here, we're off to the paddock now, have him ready for the morning." He turned and started to walk off. "Take good note of what Cookie tells you, there isn't a person this side of the black stump who knows as much about ring barking as Cookie here."

Inspirations

How often do we blame our past for the situations we are in today? Bad environment, wrong side of the tracks, never enough money, very little love. There are dozens of excuses we can find to justify our unhappy state. The fact is that these same circumstances can be and often are the building blocks to a successful and happy life. If we can accept our past as it is, and not become a victim to it, then the wisdom gained by going through these experiences will lead us to much greater heights than could otherwise have been attained. Our roots may have begun in a precariously unstable place, but acceptance in the harmony of the universe will allow us to grow toward the light.

Living in love with you eternally

Ronald Russell

Chapter Seven

Cookie's Story

Cookie led me over to his vehicle where he proceeded to scrounge around in the back, moving all kinds of interesting stuff from one side to the other, "ahh, here it is," he was pulling an old leather suitcase from under a couple of canvas haversacks. The case looked older than Cookie, and when I remarked on this, he told me that it was given to his father in appreciation of the work he had done by one of the cattle barons up north. It had been made from the cattle on the property where he worked. Beautiful carvings were carved on the supple leather and kept in this condition by years of loving care with mutton fat being rubbed into it to preserve the softness. This was a remarkable gift when we realise that indigenous persons were not considered citizens until the referendum in 1967. To me, there was a gift as well; it was the realization that many of my life lessons were being taught to me by those considered inferior by the powers to be of that era. At least the aborigines, like Cookie and Sandy were being paid the correct wage, which is more than I can say for a lot of other indigenous persons I have worked with since.

I followed cookie back to the camp fire which was being shaded from the morning sun by a large Coolabah tree, and he picked up a couple of pieces of kindling about eight inches in length. He motioned me to squat next to him and picking up my axe said while squinting along the blade, "This is a good'un, not much shoulder, we'll turn this into a gun axe." The term 'Gun' meant top or best, I was to find out later that this team of ring barkers was the 'Gun' team in the district.

Using the back of the axe he proceeded to hammer one of the pieces of kindling into the ground until there was only an inch left above ground, then placing the back of the axe against this stick he carefully measured a spot on the ground which was two thirds of the way along the axe head, he then hammered the second stick in at this point leaving it one and a half inches above the ground, he then placed the back of the axe against the lower stick and with the handle facing away from him he held it steady with his feet, this left the blade sitting on the higher stick and the sharp edge about two and a half inches above the ground. All this was achieved while sitting cross legged on the grass. Satisfied with his work so far he picked up the single cut file and dragged it across the blade in such a fashion that one stroke of the file covered the entire cutting edge of the axe. It must have taken him the best part of two hours before he was satisfied.

Patience is not one of my virtues, and having served my time as a fitter and turner, I knew that I could have done the job in ten minutes with a grinder, I told Cookie this but he just smiled "Where are you going to plug the grinder in?" he asked. "There is no power out here' he said, "and even if there was, there is none in the paddock, and that's where you'll be sharpening your axe most of the time."

Having finished with the filing, Cookie took the round stone in his hand and with the rough side, began to work it across the cutting edge in a figure eight motion; this must have taken another half hour until he finished it off with the smooth side. After testing it out by shaving a portion of his arm, he was satisfied. It had taken him at least three hours. "Look after this blade, protect it at all times, it will take you much longer to get a chip out of the blade than this did." He painfully got to his feet, "Getting old," he smiled, "Time for a cuppa, we'll finish the handle later." Over a tin pannikin 'mug' of unsweetened black tea Cookie began to tell me part of his story, he started when he and his father were on a station up near the gulf.

Apparently, Cookies dad, everyone called him Bones, came from the Gulf country and met Cookies mother while on a cattle drive down through the desert country, to Adelaide, Cookie told me that his mum travelled with Bones on all his trips throughout the desert country until she caught some kind of fever and died while Cookie was still young, maybe four or five. Bones bought Cookie up by himself keeping him by his side on all his trips, and with the help of the boss's missus got Cookie some sort of an education. He was working cattle as soon as he could ride, and became a valued Ringer 'cattle musterer' at an early age, I was a good listener and Cookie seemed to love having someone to tell his story to. Bones stayed working on that same station until he passed away in his sleep at the age of sixty two. Cookie stayed with his father until he was seventeen then left for, as he told me 'Greener pastures.' "Want another cuppa?" he asked. I nodded; I was thinking that I'm in for an interesting story here.

After pouring another mug of tea each he settled down and began his story again. "It was a lot harder to get work away from the cattle stations, well, work that paid any sort of money, at least on the stations we got a roof over our head, yeah, the money was piss poor for a blackfella on the stations, but we didn't really want for anything. It used to give me the shits though. We'd get white fellas coming out there looking for a job as ringers, knowing nothing about the country, and quite often nothing about wild cattle, and we'd have to show them the ropes while they got four times as much money as us black fellas." Cookie went into silent thought for a while, then with a smile that showed the love he had for his father, he mused, "Dad didn't mind though, when I grizzled to him about the unfairness of it all, he would shrug his shoulders and say, "we're doing alright." Cookie was getting to his feet again, "D'ya want a bit a damper to go with the cuppa?" I nodded. "Dry ok?" He asked as he returned, handing the dry damper to me as he squatted back to a comfortable position. Bloody flies get on the jam, so most of the times I take it dry, now where were we?"

"I think you are finding it hard to get work," I answered. "Oh Yeah, it wasn't hard to get work, but work where you could get a decent wage, everyone wanted to give us black bastards a job for tucker and a bit of tobacco, Ya know?" He paused for another thoughtful moment, "I never rode in the front of a truck until I started work for Scotty about fifteen years ago." He took a bite of his damper and washed it down with some tea. "It was pretty tough, we would get treated like dogs sometimes, but I've let that go a long time ago, like dad said, I'm doing alright, and besides they say what doesn't kill you, will make you stronger."

I must say that I was squirming in my seat, feeling terribly guilty about how the aboriginals were treated, sitting here as a white man being taught by a 'Black Bastard" as Cookie had called himself earlier. At least we were on the right wage now, but it would be a few years before Cookie would be treated as equal by the rest of Australia.

"Anyway," Cookie was off again, "I done alright getting the odd job mustering cattle, had a go at droving sheep too, but found it bloody boring, made a few bob around the rodeos, on both horses and bulls, that's why I'm a bit buggered now, had more than one bull stomp on me." He reached over and pored us another cup from the blackened billy sitting beside the fire.

Jimmy Sharman's boxing tent was the best money for the hours spent, and it was a fun Job as well, plenty of sheilas I'll tell you, I was pretty good with my fists in those days, and a lot of the fights were fixed to get the money in, I remember I had to cop a couple of good hidings to get the price up, but it was all in a day's work, I'll tell you this much, there's a lot of bloody good black boxers came out of Jimmy Sharman's tents, I reckon there'd be a world champ or two, but they usually ended up broke, if the piss didn't get them, rip off managers did."

"I wound up in Brisbane, nothing to do except sit in the park and drink, get in a blue here and there, got locked up once or twice, shit house life it was, and not for me. I headed out here and been in ring barking camps ever since, been cooking for about five years, too many broken bones from the good old days to keep up with these young guns today."

Cookie got to his feet and dusted his pants down. "Got a killer around the back, you can come and help me if you like; you gotta learn sometime, everyone has a turn at killing." I wasn't sure what he meant by killing, but I followed him to the bench where he picked up a sharp knife, checked the blade with his finger to see if it was sharp enough and when satisfied led me around the back of the camp to a post where a sheep was tied. "We do one of these about every five or six days, depending on how many men we have in camp, the station supplies them we just have to hang the skin for them later." It just dawned on me that this was the 'Killer' and we were going to kill it. I looked around; no gun was in sight, only the knife in Cookie's knarled hand. I was thinking "I'm not going to like this," I must have hesitated with the realization, and Cookie noticed it, "you'll get used to it, where've been killing our own food forever." With that he quickly stepped over the sheep, as though he was going to ride him, and pulling the animals head back with his left arm put the point of the knife to the sheep's neck at a point just below the right ear, "See where the knife is," Cookie was looking at me making sure I was paying attention. "We don't slice the throat as you would think, too messy, we go straight in here and out through the front, if your knife is sharp you can do it in one movement." Then pulling back on the sheep's neck he forced the knife straight through the neck and pulled it forward and out the front of the neck, keeping the neck pulled back as far as possible he allowed the sheep to bleed out, there wasn't even much fight and it was over in moments. I had made myself strong so that I wouldn't seem a wimp but it affected more than I realised, later I had my turn, more than once, but that first time is still in my mind. Cookie showed me how to "Punch" the skin off and the right way to bone the meat out. He kept the intestines and cooked them on the fire until they were crisp, handing me a piece he smiled, "This is a delicacy and belongs to whoever kills the sheep." he hung the meat in damp calico bags, there was no refrigeration in the camp, but he said it would keep for ages this way, the damp calico acted as an evaporative cooler.

Satisfied with his work he turned to me and while picking up the axe said, "We'd better get this handle finished or they'll be eating us for dinner." With that he walked over to a bin where he picked out a large glass bottle, and using the back of the axe to break it, came back to where I was sitting. He cut the handle off to about three quarters length and then proceeded to shape the handle with the broken glass, using it as you would a spoke shave, explaining that it had to be much thinner than an ordinary handle to allow the axe to be used with a flicking, rather than a chopping motion. When satisfied, he motioned me to follow him to a stand of trees about fifty yards away, "let's see how this goes," He walked up to a tree about one foot in diameter and flicked the axe into the tree at about waist height, flick, flick, flick to the right, a step to the left, flick, flick, flick to the left side and as he walked away a flick to the front to join the cuts together and then a flick to the back to complete the circular ring cut at the back, the tree was ring barked in no more than five seconds, I was amazed. "Your turn," he handed me the axe and explained the art of flicking, it looked so easy when Cookie did it, but I stuffed it completely, then after being shown a few more times I started to get the hang of it, "The secret is not to rush, you may do yourself an injury, just allow it to come to you as it comes, we won't be pushing you, we all had to learn, so take it easy to start with, you are good enough to start tomorrow. They'll be back shortly so I'd better get the tucker ready." With that Cookie went back to his fire and proceeded to stir a large pot he had simmering on the ashes beside the fire.

Inspirations

All the colours of the rainbow don't make me who I am.
Nor do any of the many religions change me.
I am much more than this,
I am the trees and stars,
I am the earth I walk upon,
I am the streams in which I swim,
and the air I breath,
To label myself in any way,
separates me from that which I really am,
and that is the omnipresent, omniscient and omnipotent
oneness of love.

Living in Love with you eternally

Ronald Russell   Namaste'

Chapter Eight

After a hearty breakfast of lamb chops, Eggs, baked beans and damper we climbed on to the back of the truck and headed out to the paddock in which we were working.

There was a line of ring barked trees about one hundred yards long. I was placed in the middle of this line, even though it was early, the day was already warming up and I was dressed the same as the other workers, stubby shorts and sandshoes, no shirt or hat. I was told to always stay in the middle of the cut trees, this way those working either side of me could cut some of my trees allowing me to keep up.

I've never seen anyone work so fast as these boys, we were really men but we called ourselves boys. They would cut each tree in the same fashion as I was taught, but actually ran between trees, and they kept this pace up for two hours until the smoko break where Scottie had the billy boiling and a slice of damper and jam if you wanted it.

Already my hands were becoming covered in blisters even between my fingers, and by lunch time I was in so much pain I was seriously thinking of quitting, thinking that this isn't white man's work. I confided these thoughts to Sandy and he just laughed, "I've been waiting for this, I thought you would have said something at smoko," "I was going to, but I was too ashamed, seeing you put me up for the job and all, it's much worse now though, I can hardly hold the axe." Sandy took me aside so the others wouldn't hear us. "You are doing really well, and doing a good job of keeping up, just before you go back after lunch, pee on your hands, this heals the blisters and keeps the skin soft, Then grab the axe tightly until the next break, do the same again for the last two hours, then the same again tomorrow starting just before work." I looked at him doubtfully, "You are having a lend of me, aren't you?" Sandy smiled and showed me his hands, just like mine only where I had blisters he had calluses, "It'll probably take a week but you'll feel better after tomorrow."

Over time I got to be a pretty good axeman, and really enjoyed the job, no trouble keeping up, and got on with everyone. They called me Gubby. A decade or two ago Gubby would have been a derogatory name; it is short for Government man, or white man from the Guberment. These government police and other agents only spelt trouble for the aboriginals, rounding them up and separating families, but that seemed to be mainly in the past, in this area anyway, and Gubby became a nickname for white friends.

The dry heat wasn't as burning to the skin as the salty heat of the coast, and I was getting a very good tan, I think I was darker than Sandy, but I'm paying for my life in the sun today, fifty years down the track, skin cancers all over, but that's life.

I'm really grateful for the times I had with these men of the land, they showed me a way of living with nature that I never thought possible, and I'm afraid may not be possible today.

Sunday was our day off and we would head over to the next paddock where a large dam took up quite a few acres of the property. The dam was well stocked with Yellow Belly, a tasty fresh water fish similar to Perch, and Yabbies, a type of fresh water Cray fish. The fish were thrown onto the coals of our camp fire just as they came from the water, no scaling skinning or gutting, it only took about five minutes and they were removed and opened up, the gut had shrunk to a small ball which was discarded and the juicy white flesh was eaten off the skin from the inside out. The fat in the head and around the eyes was considered a real delicacy, the Cray were cooked in much the same way.

Being brought up in this environment they were at home with all kinds of wild life, and seemed to be able to find it everywhere. I remember one day I was called over to a large tree, and they pointed to a branch about ten feet from the ground, Damma, one of the younger boys, explained that this branch had a native bee hive in it, he explained that although it didn't look hollow from the ground, you could tell by the way the leaves were a lot more scarce than the leaves on the other branches, when he got me to look closer I could see the tiny black bees entering a hole along the branch. "How do you get the honey I asked?" Damma smiled, "We won't be getting any today but when it is high like this we usually cut the branch down, and it's dying anyway." They showed me how to find and cut Witchetty Grubs from trees where they had bored their holes, and to cook them on a handful of dry grass for a few seconds until the skin was crisp, it took a bit of courage to get the first one down, but I used my trusty reasoning, 'if they can do it, so can I.' Witchetty Grubs are very nice on toast.

There was a large hole dug beside the camp fire and I was to find out that this was the oven they used while relaxing on Sundays. Over a period of months I was to experience the flavours of an array of bush tucker that the boys caught.

Part of the camp fire coals were thrown into the hole followed by some river stones they had stored nearby, then whatever animal they had captured would be gutted and thrown in on top of the stones, a sheet of corrugated iron was placed over the hole and more coals placed on top, After a few hours the iron would be removed and the juicy morsels divided around, I was to experience the flavours of, snake, kangaroo, wild pig, porcupine, Goanna, and a few birds such as plain turkey and some water birds. Often these were cooked along with wild herbs thrown in to enhance the flavour. Sundays they explained, were their back to culture days, or back to their Earth mother. I think this culture has been mostly lost these days, maybe because there isn't much natural environment left. A lot of the country we were ring barking ended up as a dust bowl, and at times, years later, one could see the dust being blown away by large dust storms, taking hundreds of tons of top soil and dumping it into the sea.

We went to a different town for our break, and as usual went to the pub to cash our checks, the publican looked us over and said to me "I'll cash yours but I want those black bastards out of here and take that yella fella out too." You could have knocked me over with a feather, I started to react but Sandy pulled me aside, "let it go, I'll explain outside," the others had already left but not before sending a couple of racist remarks back to the publican. "Who does that white trash think he is, calling us black bastards, we did nothing wrong," this was coming from one of the younger members, he was pretty riled up.

Once outside, Sandy explained. "About six months ago, we were all drinking in this hotel when half a dozen white ringers from a property up north came into the pub, a fight broke out over a pool game and the pub got badly damaged, we got the blame, probably because we were black and were easier to blame, I don't know but we haven't been allowed back since, should've given it a wide berth this time as well, there's another pub up the road and we are always welcome there, although you might feel a little uncomfortable, not many white fellas drink there." I laughed, "I'd rather drink with you black bastards anywhere than with that white trash down the road, any way what's this yella fella stuff, does that worry you?" Sandy was thoughtful for a bit, "no, not much these days, you know it means half caste, don't you." This was more a statement than a question. "No, it used to worry me when I was younger, especially at school where I got teased by both blacks and whites, got into a lot of fights over it, Leah got into a bit of trouble too, but mainly from the girls and I think that was because she was good looking rather than being half caste." We've both let it go now, but it pops up sometimes, especially when there's conflict between black and white, I feel like I've got to take sides," he was smiling now, "I suppose I go with the underdog and that's usually the black fella."

It was two months before I got back to the river camp to see Leah, and another two months before we were back again, I had saved quite a bit of money and was really happy to see Leah. We cashed our checks, and headed down to the river camp with our usual cartons of beer.

I was laughing and joking with mum, and felt in a wonderful light mood, but I sensed a distance happening with Leah, I put it down to being away for two months, and thought that a couple of beers would loosen us up.

I suppose it was a couple of hours later when one of the fellas from the other end of the camp started to niggle me, I found out later that he had been sleeping with Leah and resented my involvement with her. The last thing I wanted was a fight, especially as I was a guest, but he kept on at me. I was thinking about going over to the pub to sleep when he king hit me, it really shook me, but as it turned out it was the silliest thing he could have done. There is something in me that frightens me, once I'm hit I lose it completely, it's as though some prehistoric energy takes over, and I automatically go into attack mode, I have no control, I just unconsciously lash out, Dave, that was his name was laying on the ground blood pouring from his nose and mouth and I was still punching him as I started to come to my senses, I could hear myself saying "I'm going to kill this bastard, I'm going to kill him." They were pulling me off as Dave's mother came onto the scene and saw Dave laying there covered in blood. She started to attack me but the others were holding her. "You fucking white trash, come here to fuck our women, she was fuming, then she turned to Leah's mum, and you're fucking worse, you go away and fuck some white trash and make two yella fellas then bring them here for this white trash to fuck and make more," with that she spat at Leah's mum as they took her away.

All went silent, I was terribly embarrassed, I apologised to everyone and left for the pub. Leah came over the next day and after an in depth discussion, we decided to call our relationship off, I mean you could hardly call it a relationship, Just a few one or two night stands whenever I came to town, even though it seemed like more than that to me. That was the last time I saw Leah, and two months later I headed off to greener pastures, as Cookie would call it.

Brisbane was the closest large city, and I found myself drinking in the parks with my indigenous friends, I had plenty of money so I was accepted readily, and it wasn't long before I got a taste for port wine, 'Plonk.' After a couple of months of this I knew what Cookie had been talking about, when he said he found it boring and that he felt that it was a place without hope, I realised I was better than this, although twenty years down the track this is exactly where I ended up, and there wasn't a choice any longer. For now I had a choice and headed back out west.

Inspirations

*There are times when I sit quietly under a shady tree,
peering with squinted eyes west toward the orange and opal
hues of the setting sun.
The same sun that is setting over the beloved outback
Australia I so love.
There is a pain in my heart because I know that old
Australia is no longer there.
Then old Sunny boy,
the Golden Labrador comes up beside me,
and licks at my hand,
just to let me know he is there,
our eyes meet and for a moment we are one.
The moment passes, but is not lost,
my heart begins to sing and
I know all is right in Gods world.*

Living in Love with you eternally

Ronald Russell   Namaste'

Chapter Nine

One of the largest cattle stations, smack bang in the middle of the Northern Territory was my next port of call, and because I was a fitter and turner it was fairly easy to get a job as a windmill mechanic. It's funny how things seem to happen at the right time if you are aware, I had just pulled into a road house for a bite to eat, and got talking with a couple of blokes about work, "there's plenty of ringing work around," a tall slim cattleman was saying, and I think Charlie is leaving his job just up the road, he's a windmill mechanic, what do you do?" He was looking directly into my eyes, I felt as though I was being evaluated as to whether I was good enough for this area. I had never worked with cattle, and as this was purely cattle country I decided not to bullshit and tell the truth, "Haven't had anything to do with cattle, just come up from ring barking along the Queensland New South Wales border, I reckon I could do the windmill mechanic work if I was shown the ropes. I'm a fitter by trade."

I was given directions to the station where Charlie was working, and after a few more beers headed out. It was early afternoon when I arrived, and a couple of aboriginal women carrying washing in cane baskets pointed my way to the office.

They were very happy to have me to replace Charlie as it was in the middle of the dry season and quite a few mills were down. I was given a room in the stockman's quarters and then introduced to Charlie, the mechanic I was to be replacing, he showed me around and told me that I would be starting at seven in the morning, and that he would be leaving the same afternoon.

That evening, after a wonderful steak dinner, I confided in Charlie that I knew nothing about windmills. He laughed "You know that they go round and round with the wind don't you?" He didn't wait for an answer and went on "That's all you need to know for now, I take it you can drive a truck, the boys will do the rest, they're the best windmill mechanics this side of the black stump, wherever that is."

The next morning I was given a tabletop truck, and Charlie introduced me to Sydney and Bungy, my two aboriginal helpers. Charlie jumped into the passenger seat while Sydney and Bungy climbed onto the back.

After about thirty minutes driving along unsealed roads we pulled up at the bore that needed repair. This consisted of a large wheel, with blades forty feet in circumference, fixed to a frame approximately sixty feet high. This frame stood over the bore which was an eight inch hole drilled to a depth of one hundred and eighty feet, this was lined with a galvanised sleeve, and inside this was a five inch casing in which the water was brought to the surface by a ball valve pump connected to the mill by steel rods. When the water arrived at the top of the casing it was diverted into holding tanks and water troughs for the cattle. This mill was turning but no water was coming out. Both Sydney and Bungy had gone to the mill and put their ear to the steel casing, then after a short moment called to Charlie, "She's got a hole in the casing near the bottom." Charlie was satisfied with that, "We'll check a couple of others then call it a day, I'm off to Darwin this arvo."

The next day the two blackfellas jumped onto the back of the truck and we headed out to the bores, I had a list of which ones needed attention, but I relied on Sydney and Bungy to select the order in which they were to be fixed.

We pulled up to the first bore that we had looked at yesterday, and after my two offsiders had unloaded some gear from the truck they asked me to back the truck up to the base of the frame. "That'll do" Sydney was already climbing the frame with some rope to tie the blade off so that it couldn't spin while we were working on the mill, and Bungy was fixing pulley blocks to the frame. I felt at a total loss, I had no idea whatsoever as to what was happening, when, almost as though he had read my mind, Bungy called out "You just stay by the truck and be ready to drive it forward and back as we ask you, but first of all, turn the truck around and bring the bull bar up close to the frame here," He was pointing to a concrete pier that the mill frame was bolted to. "If you like, while we get this gear in place you could light up a fire and get the billy on; we'll start pulling the rods after smoko." Bungy spoke in a humble way and I didn't feel at all like he was ordering me about, actually he spoke the same way to Sydney, Bungy was apparently the more experienced worker here and automatically assumed leadership of this small team.

During smoko, this consisted of black unsweetened tea and damper; I asked how they knew what was wrong with the bore, Sydney spoke up "We listen to the sounds coming from down the bore, if we put our ear against the casing, we can tell where the problem is." "This sounds like blackfella magic to me," I was genuinely surprised. They both Laughed, "Come on, well show you," Bungy was already climbing the frame where the mill had been tied off, and undoing the holding rope, set the mill wheel in motion. Sydney beckoned me across to where he had his ear to the casing. "Put your ear against this and tell me what you hear." I did what I was told and listened carefully, not knowing what to expect, I told him that all I could hear was working noises of the rods going up and down and clunking sounds, they meant nothing to me. "The clunking sound you hear is the ball valve opening and closing as the rod goes up and down, we'll show you later when we get it out, now listen again, can you hear a hissing sound as the rod comes up?" after a while I could just hear what I would call a very quiet whooshing as the rod came toward the top of its stroke. "Yes, I think I've got it, what's it mean?" by this time Bungy had joined us and said "that hissing sound you hear is water escaping from a hole in the casing, probably where the first casing ends, the hole is caused by electrolysis attacking the casing just above the water line, usually around the thread of the casing, by the sound of it the hole is probably a bit bigger than a two bob bit. (Twenty cents)

I was amazed; these two had done very little schooling, if any, and were using words like electrolysis, and they were envisioning things happening one hundred and eighty feet below the surface, "Like I said; Blackfella magic."

"We'd better get this thing pulled;" Bungy was already on his way to the top to tie the blade off, and Sydney was threading a wire rope through the pulley blocks and connecting it to the bull bar in the front of the truck. "Were going to pull the rods first," Bungy informed me, as we undo the rods you take up the slack in the rope by driving the truck back, we'll unscrew the first rod then you back up until it is free of the casing we'll clamp the remaining rods off then you take the free rod away and well lay it beside the frame over there," he was pointing to a cleared area that had obviously been used before for this purpose. "Your job is to follow my hand signals, back up, stop, and come forward, ok?"

There were nine, twenty foot rods and the ball valve came up with the last rod. Bungy called me over and showed me how the valve worked, as the rod went down into the water the ball was forced up away from its bottom seal, allowing water into the casing, as the rod came up the ball closed against its seal and the water was lifted further up the casing, this continued with each turn of the wheel until the casing was full of water where it was directed off to a storage tank and watering trough for the cattle. "Now you can see how a hole in the casing allows the water to escape before it reaches the top." Bungy was fitting a clamp to the top of the casing, "We'll pull this tomorrow, this is enough for today, and we can pick up a new casing when we get back to the station, all ready for tomorrow."

Next morning, I ate my breakfast with the ringers at the station mess, while Sydney and Bungy ate at their respective homes. We loaded a couple of casings onto the truck; the second was a spare just in case the hole was at the thread joining the two bottom casings. At the bore, the two boys jumped off and Bungy directed me to drive the truck into the same position as before. They hooked up the rope, and we began pulling the casings from the bore, when we got to the last one bungy called me across to see the hole, just below the thread on the last length of casing. "There you are, just like we said." He was inspecting the other casing that screwed into this one, "Hasn't affected this length, just need to replace the one today." He was fixing the clamp to the new casing, "We'll have some lunch and get these casings back before we knock off this arvo, that'll leave us an easy day tomorrow replacing the rods and greasing the mill."

The next day after all the rods were in place and while sitting on a log drinking a cuppa after lunch in the shade of a lonely tree I decided to bring up the thing that had been bothering me since the first day.

I asked Sydney "Why do you blokes always ride in the back of the truck, especially when there's a bit of rain about like the other day, I know it wasn't much, but I'm surprised you didn't jump in the front?"

Sydney looked uncomfortable and glanced across to Bungy who wasn't looking much better, I thought I'd help them out, "Is it because you like the fresh air and don't like the fumes in the truck?"

Bungy finally answered "it's company policy that we ride in the back, not just on this station but all the stations around here." I don't know what it was, but I could feel the heat start to rise from my stomach, I suppose I knew that this was the reason; after all, Cookie had told me that he hadn't ridden in the front of a truck until he worked with Scotty.

Here I was, a white man in a foreign environment with two older, and in my opinion much superior persons, who were teaching me how to do a job that they had been doing for years, men who knew the ins and outs of this country like no other, and were more than willing to share their extensive knowledge.

Oh, I had heard stories, and I remembered Mr and Mrs Jones from my childhood, and the pub we got barred from last year. The unfairness hit me, "Fuck them, I blurted out, I'm not driving any truck if my friends can't share a seat in the front with me, and I'll fucking well tell them when I get back too.

Both Sydney and Bungy looked uncomfortable, "I wouldn't do that." It was Sydney who spoke first. "It wouldn't go down real well," I didn't give him a chance to finish I was riled, "It'll go down the way it fucken goes down, this can't go on, besides I feel bloody uncomfortable sitting in the front while you two bastards have to ride in the back."

There was no offence taken at the word bastard, it was taken as it was said, in a friendly way. Bungy spoke up next "Just calm down for a bit old mate, we have it pretty good." He had that calm authoritive voice one listens to. We have a house each for our families, food and a bit of spending money left over, they hold some back for the wet season when we can't work, it all works out in the end." He thought for a while. "It's been company policy for a long while that we ride in the back, we don't mind, I suppose we're used to it, and it's not just on this property."

Bungy had succeeded in calming me down, but I still felt guilty allowing these men show me the ropes when I was getting four times as much pay as they were. I knew that they didn't want me to take it further so I changed the subject back to the mill.

A few months further on, and I had become a proficient windmill mechanic, and could almost hold my own with Sydney and Bungy, although I would still do as they suggested, they had trained me well. The wet was almost upon us and when it hit properly work would cease for a couple of months.

The months leading up to the wet were very dry; the grass would crackle under foot where it was short. Fires were the big danger now and we were on the lookout for them twenty four seven. Some of the nearby stations were having trouble and the sunsets were a mixture of beautiful mauves and reds due to the smoke from the fires. We were told that it wouldn't be a matter of if, but when the fires hit. We carried diesel fire lighters so that we could back burn when necessary. When the fires started, all work ceased and all hands were put to fighting fires. The country was so dry that the fires almost started of their own accord. The heat from the fires would cause Willy Willies and these would lift the fire across the fire breaks and sometimes start new fires hundreds of yards away. This was a very dangerous time and we had to be very careful that the fire didn't cut us off.

There was one paddock probably about five miles long by half a mile wide, and while we were driving down the boundary road we noticed a fire start up about five hundred yards behind us, we were doing thirty miles an hour and before we had gone another half a mile the fire was upon us, looking across at it, it seemed to be at least fifteen above the three foot high grass, rolling along like a fiery rolled up carpet, giving the impression that the grass under it wouldn't be burnt. What was actually happening was the grass in front of the fire was getting so hot that it was giving off gas and the clear space we could see between the fire and the grass was this gas and as the rolling carpet of fire passed all that remained was blackened earth and a few animals that had been caught by the speed of the fire, after seeing this I had a new and much greater respect for fire. The fires kept up until the wet season put them out, such is the life in the Territory.

One day we were out in the paddock when we had what is called a cloudburst, the water came down in bucket loads; it was so heavy we couldn't see ten feet in front of us, I made the boys get in the front while we rode the storm out, and then after it had passed, Sydney who had wandered off into the paddock called us over to where he was picking up silver things from the grass. "Fish" he called out, "Fish, it's raining fish." We ran to him, and sure enough there were small silver fish all over the ground. The only way they could have got there was in the rain, I had heard of this before but never really believed it. I still wasn't too sure, but I couldn't see any other explanation.

Dry river beds began to run and flow over the roads, small fish would swim upstream and seemingly travel uphill over small water falls to get to deeper water where they were caught by the boys and me with small silver pins bent into hooks tied to a piece of string, no bait was needed, the fish were so hungry they would go for the silver pin as though it was the last thing to eat on the planet, the glittering silver pin must have looked like small fish to them.

We were told that it was flooding up in the gulf country, and that it would take about three weeks to reach us. The land was so flat, that when the water escaped from the water ways, it completely covered all remaining ground, there was very little high ground, and the cattle had already been moved to these areas.

The work came to an end for a couple of months because we couldn't travel on the roads any longer.

The aboriginal families were packed up and transported, along with their belongings to the main highway, where they stayed in makeshift tent camps beside a roadhouse; they were to stay there for the couple of months of the wet season.

It didn't look very comfortable from where I stood, and I heard that their money would run out before they got back to the station, with quite a large bill owing to the roadhouse.

I had made friends with an aboriginal ringer who was nicknamed Hoppy, because of his limp due to a rodeo accident, they reckon he could ride any bull on the station, and was just as good with the horses; he was the same age as me and could fight like a thrashing machine. That's how we became friends. A mob of us had travelled along with a mob from the adjoining station to Mt. Isa where we proceeded to get enough Dutch courage to pick up one of the many girls out looking for a good time with the men from the Territory, who, for a short time at least had plenty of money to throw around.

Hoppy and I had somehow cottoned onto the same girl, and she was in her glory, two men vying after her charms, this was the sixties in Mt. Isa, and we were in the Snake pit, an infamous bar in one of the many hotels in town, but one of the few where blacks could drink. It was disco night, and both Hoppy and I were drinking rum, quite a lot of rum. I don't remember how the fight started, but I remember being hit half a dozen times in succession, and going down in a barrage of punches, lucky I was pretty drunk so I didn't feel the pain, I only knew that I was in a fight and had to get up. Hoppy was dancing around waiting until I was on my feet, it was like that in those days, fights were pretty clean, no hitting or kicking the one who was down.

He came at me again but the adrenalin had sobered me up enough to protect myself and even get a couple of punches in myself, he went down once but somehow I knew he was the better fighter, we had been fighting for about fifteen minutes and were both covered in blood when I was saved by the police coming in and breaking us up, we both spent the night in the lockup. The next day found us drinking together, licking our wounds and congratulating each other on a good fight; we had become very good friends. I stayed in Mt. Isa for about three weeks and in that time I had sex three times, had two fights, got locked up three times and spent well over a thousand dollars. ??????

Inspirations

*It is when we become vulnerable
that we find our true self
This takes courage and trust
It is only when the masks are removed
And the truth revealed
That we can play openly with others
In the freedom of the spirit.*

Living in Love with you eternally

Ronald Russell   Namaste

Chapter Ten

Time to leave I reckon, I headed toward Darwin but ended up in Katherine, and heard about a mechanics job on a station near Timber Creek, a small town west of Katherine. I had my tools with me and got a bit of spare cash from fixing a couple of cars up for the locals.

It wasn't too long before I linked up with one of the girls from the black camp on the other side of the river, and was again welcomed into her family. This lasted for a few weeks until the manager of the station near Timber Creek came to collect me to work on his vehicles.

What a fabulous job, I was my own boss, just had to keep the machinery going. Weekends off, freedom to do whatever I wished. I don't know if any of the readers have seen the movie Jedda? It's a love story of an aboriginal couple, probably set in the early part of last century, the scenery is out of this world, high rainbow coloured cliffs, looking down on a crystal clear river winding its way through amazing gorges filled with fish and abounding in wild animal life. This 'Jedda' country was my weekend play ground.

When there was no mechanical work I helped out with the general station work, which consisted of mustering the cattle, branding and bull catching.

I had never been bull catching, or even seen bulls caught the way these boys were doing it. The bulls they were after had probably never seen a human up close; they were completely wild, always staying in among the timber, and were too dangerous to catch on horseback.

The station owned an old ex army four wheel drive Jeep, open at the top with the doors removed for easy access and exit. A very heavy bull bar was fitted to the front and stayed back to the chassis, it was a solid piece of machinery, and it needed to be.

The boys would chase the wild bull through the bush with the jeep until they got it out into the open, once in the open they would get the jeep just behind the bulls rump and start pushing, this was all happening at full speed, as soon as the bull started to turn to escape, the driver sped up causing the bull to lose its balance and fall to on its side, the jeep would keep on going until the bull was caught under the bull bar with the weight of the jeep holding it down, the passenger would then quickly jump out and tie the legs of the bull. The cattle truck, which I was allowed to drive, was driven up to the bull and the bull was winched onto the back of the truck ready for market. Sometimes the role was reversed when the bull outsmarted the driver and started chasing the open jeep, I found this to be quite amusing, but the boys were very experienced and sometimes the passenger would jump from the jeep and grab the bull's tail and run to the side, again causing the bull to lose balance, the driver had to be quick to get the jeep onto the bull before he got to his feet.

There was a governess at this station; her job was to teach the children who lived here, and, like me, when she wasn't teaching she would be out mustering or doing other work with the cattle. I was there at the time when Julie the governess was to marry Jim the jackaroo; they were both in their early thirties and were getting married on the station.

My experience came in handy when they asked me to cook the pig in the ground; During the week before the wedding, I had the boys dig a shallow hole, and the day before the wedding, we lit a large hardwood fire in it, after it had turned to coals we put river rocks on to heat up and covered this with another fire which we kept burning all night.

We went fishing as well on the day before, and managed to catch a couple of large barramundi. I decided to fillet one and make raw fish by slicing the fish into thin slices and placing them in a large jar of vinegar along with sliced tomatoes and onion. The other fish was exceptionally large, over a meter long and weighed fifty five pound. We decided to cook this in the fire along with the pig, but for a much shorter time.

On the wedding day we stuffed the pig with vegetables and sewed the gut up, we even had an apple for its mouth; the fish was prepared in a similar way, no apple though. The pig and the fish were wrapped in banana leaves and the pig was placed in the coals under the river stones which had been raked to the side and then placed back on top of the pig, the coals were raked back onto the stones and a fire was started again on these.

We were finished by nine in the morning, so that left us nine hours to cook the pig and have it ready for the feast at six; I decided to give the fish two hours in a cooler part of the fire.

You have no idea how proud I felt when all three dishes worked out perfectly, the raw fish was a big hit, and I allowed some of the guests to sample the fat from the fish head and from around the eyes. The juicy flesh lifted off the skin in perfect sized portions. And the pig, it looked amazing when it was unwrapped and placed onto fresh banana leaves complete with the apple still in place. I was thinking that it's a pity we didn't have a snake to serve in the same way, the way the guests took to this food I'm sure a snake would have gone down very well.

Inspirations

Moment of doubt

As I begin writing this I am experiencing doubt as to whether I am a good enough writer, know enough descriptive words, have enough education. I also know from experience that as I write this, I will discover the truth. As I stand back and observe the big picture, I see clearly who and what I am. The Poem, Desiderata tells me, I'm a child of the universe, no less than the trees and stars, and I have a right to be here. I see humbly the gifts I have received, the gift to be able to walk with others less fortunate and share this wonderful gift of love, simply, with a smile, a kind word or loving hug. As I write I see the beautiful poetry my friends share, Humility returns, that is their gift, I have mine. There is something inside of me that calls on me to write what I write, without fear, to live as I live, without fear. Because this is who I am.

Living in Love with you eternally.

Ronald Russell   Namaste'

Chapter Eleven

After a few months, I again got itchy feet and decided to head towards Darwin, but got on the piss in Katherine and somehow ended up in Mount Isa where I got a job as a maintenance fitter in the mine.

Working as a leading hand fitter in Mount Isa, hating the responsibility, drinking to relieve the pressure, and living in a 'donga' in the scorching heat of a north west Queensland summer, can't wait to leave, breathing in lead fumes from the smelter over which I was working. Hans, a German fitter working alongside me is telling me he is going back to sea. My ears prick up. The call of the sea again. "How do you go to sea, what do you have to do to get on a ship, could I get a job on a ship?" I'm becoming excited; I've got a thousand questions to ask. "Easy, it's really easy; they have trouble getting experienced men in the engine room." "I'm not experienced." My heart dropped. "Yes you are, you're a fitter the same as me, I didn't know anything before I caught my first ship, Scandinavian ships are the best, I came here on a Swedish ship, and just signed off in Brisbane before coming here." "Do you think they would take me?" "Have you got a passport?" "No, are they hard to get?" I don't know anything about travelling overseas, my trip to NZ wasn't any different to travelling to another city in Australia. "Probably take a few weeks, in the meantime you can get your medical and inoculations, you should be at sea within four to six weeks, although that depends on a ship being available, I'm leaving next Friday, come with me and I'll show you the ropes. They start you as a motor apprentice, and train you to becoming a motorman which is the same as an engineer on Australian ships, I'm still a motor apprentice, and it's about the same pay as you get here."

Brisbane back in the sixties, was more like a large regional city rather than the capital of Queensland, and there wasn't a lot of difference between the city people and the country folk, the dividing line between the culture of the city and bush was blurred, and it wasn't odd to see men and women wearing the country clothes, of Stetson, jeans and riding boots around town.

It was in this setting, that, with the aid of my German mate, I strolled into the Swedish consulate and applied for a position on a Swedish ship. I was surprised at the ease and laid back relaxed attitude of the consulate. He had the accent of what I thought the accent of a Swede would be, and a funny thing, he even looked like what I thought a Swede would look like, fair hair and all.

After viewing my papers he sat back and calmly told me that there would be a ship waiting for me as soon as I had my passport and inoculations in order. It was that easy, you would think new seamen were walking in there every day looking for work, I was to find out later that Australia was a popular place for the Swedes to disembark, jobs were easy to get on shore, and they could have a great working holiday here. Many ended up married to Aussie girls and stayed to raise their families.

I decided to take my German mate down to Musgrave Park to meet my old drinking mates, many were still there, and were happy to see me again, especially seeing I had a carton of port wine under my arm.

The first hour or so was great, a lot of laughter and good old Australian teasing and ribbing of each other, but I noticed a distance growing between the park inhabitants and my German mate, maybe he didn't understand Aussie humour, I don't know, but he was getting increasingly drunk, and with the drunkenness came the arrogance, and this was not a place to fall out with the locals, better men than us have lost their lives here.

"Come on Hans," I suggested, "let's get back to our hotel, it's getting late. Hans shook my arm away, "These Schwartz Negers won't make me leave." He was about to say more but he was sat on his rump by a punch to the jaw which came from nowhere, even though I wasn't directly involved I knew that this was a very dangerous situation for me as well as Hans. When colour gets mixed up with drink anything can happen, luckily the punch had sobered Hans enough to see the predicament he was in, and I don't suppose he felt so superior, looking up from his sitting position on the ground at half a dozen angry black faces. He mumbled something under his breath as he was rising, but stopped from saying anything out loud when again confronted by the angry faces. I managed to get him away, in one piece, and he left on a ship two days later.

I decided not to visit the park again, but it was only a couple of days before I was back there drinking with the boys. It doesn't seem to matter how seriously I try to stop drinking, after a couple of drinks I just seem to lose control of how many I have and what company I keep, I suppose that is one reason why I like to go out west where there is no daily alcohol available.

It was six weeks before I was ready to go to sea, and in that time I had been in quite a few fights, locked up a few times and had spent almost all my money.

It was a real blessing when I got my passport and the consulate sent me off to Port Kembla to catch my first ship, I had a beautiful Blonde wood Levine Guitar, That I had had since I was sixteen years old, I had tried to learn to play it many times but I'm afraid I have no ear for music, It's funny, I really love music, and can tell when someone else is out of tune, but can't hold a tune myself, anyway I was pretty broke so I pawned it for fifty pound, I didn't want to go to sea without any money.

I spent a few days in Port Kembla, drinking in the seaman's bars, getting to know the feel of the port life, I didn't want to look too much like a new comer, fortunately, my experience in Garden Island and especially the pubs in Littleton NZ helped me out. The excitement was running through my veins, as I climbed a little unsteadily up the wobbly gang way onto my first ever deep sea ship, and a foreign one at that.

I had thought language would be a problem, but it turned out that most of the crew had learned English at school and had plenty of practice while sailing into English speaking ports.

My duties at the start were to wake the watchmen up for their shift, then tidy their cabin and make their bed, and then clean the toilets and bathroom. I was shown how to do this by another motorman, everything had to be spotless and the bed made to hospital standard. That's one thing I'll say about this Swedish ship, it was the cleanest, and most efficient ship I have worked on.

There are very large waves at times outside Port Kembla, which roll toward the shore from east to west, we were sailing north so the waves were hitting us side on, and on my second day, I found myself watching the pitch indicator on the front bulk head with more than a little concern. This consisted of a quadrant marked with red at each side, as the ship rolled sideway the pendulum would swing toward the red marks, and it seemed to be getting closer to the red on each successive roll. "What happens if the pendulum hits the red marks?" I was getting a little worried. "It's called the death roll." Lars the head motorman explained. "When the pendulum goes into the red zone, we have to leave the engine room, just in case the ship rolls right over." I don't know to this day if that is true, but I can tell you that whenever I was in the engine room during rough weather I kept a very good watch on that pendulum.

The Pacific Ocean is well named, quiet glassy seas most of the way over to Los Angeles, via the Gilbert islands and Honolulu. I was a little disappointed with Honolulu, I had expected to see an island with coconuts and grass skirted girls, living in grass huts on the beautiful beaches. Instead I saw sky scrapers and the only grass skirts were on the girls doing performances for tourists. After Los Angeles, we unloaded at San Francisco, where Lars hired a Mustang convertible, and took me for a tour of the city. Driving on the right hand side was frightening for me, especially since Lars had a lead foot and was intent on showing me just how fast this Mustang could go. I enjoyed eating the crabs cooked in boilers on Fishermans Wharf, and rode the cable car down the very steep hill which led to the wharf. I checked out Ripley's' Believe It or Not, but the thing that impressed most were the bars. Australia to my knowledge was five to ten years behind them. They were small plush carpeted areas, very cosy with lots of neon signage, many had partly dressed women, some serving, others dancing in cages suspended from the darkened roof by gold chains. An absolutely amazing atmosphere.

Portland Oregon was experiencing a lot of racial tension when we arrived and the crew was advised not to go ashore, although we weren't prevented from going. Lars and I decided to have a look around, and as usual entered the first bar off the wharf. The bar was full of black drinkers, but I didn't notice this, and walked straight to the bar and ordered a drink. "Sorry, but you can't drink here." I was taken back and responded a little angrily, "Why not, what's wrong with me?" It was then that I noticed the silence that had fallen over the room and looked at the faces, all watching me. Lars had me by the arm and was pulling me back toward the door, just as another drinker came right up to my face and said, "Might be a good idea if you go with your friend." Then I was out the door and beating a hurried retreat back to the ship, but not before passing a crowd of about eight or ten black men, standing around on an opposite corner, I could feel the tension in the air, and was glad to get back to the safety of the ship. It was not long after this that we heard Portland was set on fire.

We loaded timber in Coos bay, then sailed inside Vancouver Island to the city of Vancouver, probably the most beautiful harbour I have sailed into, possibly with the exception of Sydney Harbour. I'll never forget the magic of those Pacific Ocean voyages and the abundant see life, with seals frolicking in the calm waters, and dolphins or porpoises, riding the bow waves for endless miles. The flying fish landing on the deck when it got a little choppy and the mighty wingspan of the majestic albatross as it glides only feet above the waves in its seemingly endless search for food.

On one trip we carried Rising Fast, a very famous Australian racehorse to America. I sailed that route or similar routes seven times before I signed off in Newcastle to spend some time with my family. Rita had just got married and had a baby boy; Mum and dad were just the same and seemed happy enough. I got a job back building wheat silos. Only this time I was to go out to the wheat growing areas around Dubbo in western NSW and erect and install the wheat handling equipment on site. A pretty cushy job, living first class in the local hotels, all found. We were about three weeks into the job when the leading hand, Ken, called us over, telling us we were going to have an early smoko. I was walking back to the smoko shed alongside Ken, when I had the thought that Mum had died. Out of the blue I turned to Ken and asked "Did my mum just die?" he looked at me in shock. "How did you know that?" he asked, shaking his head in disbelief. "That's why we are having an early smoko, so that I could break the news gently." I don't know how I knew, as far as I knew mum wasn't sick at all, at least no more than her usual migraine attacks, which used to put her into a dark room for a few days. There was always that bond between mum and me, and now it carried over a distance of five hundred miles give or take a few. I remember the darkened funeral parlour, and seeing the coffin sitting there, I don't remember anything else other than an idea we were at a cemetery not far from home overlooking the ocean. I don't remember another thing about the funeral, not even who was there, it's strange, but I can't see another human being at that funeral, Not even dad or my sister Rita. And I have never been back to that grave which I can't remember seeing either. I must have blocked it all out. I still don't know what mum died from, even though Rita has told me more than once, I do remember that it took me three days to cry, I had to sit quietly and let myself go, the feeling of self pity over came me and the healing tears came, and I clearly remember thinking what a relief it was to finally cry.

Inspirations

God is not a being but a state of being
Look only for the good in all things
As we look upon the world
With Love, Kindness and Compassion
Then through grace,
We become these values,
It is a wonderful world.

Living in Love with you eternally

Ronald Russell   Namaste

Chapter Twelve

There was a bulk carrier in Newcastle loading Coal for Japan, a large ship in those days, 50, 000 tons. Dad was grieving mum and I was finding him hard to live with, we were both drinking to extreme, so I decided to get a job on the bulk carrier, I said my goodbyes and sailed within the week.

Although being Norwegian owned, it was a Panamanian registered ship. They got away with a lot of safety, and other rules by registering under Panamanian registration. It was called a black ship, and when I enquired as to what the 'Black' stood for, it was explained that the crew was made up of many who for one reason or another could not work on regular ships, and alcohol was limited to two small bottles of beer each a week. There was probably more alcohol aboard that ship than the rest of the Norwegian fleet. They even had a home brew going inside the funnel. It was stored under bunks and in cupboards, and as far as the powers to be were concerned it was not unusual to see empty bottles being thrown overboard from the top deck where the Captain and Chief engineer were partying on.

There were chunks out of the rubberised deck which covered the passages on our deck, and when I asked what had caused this, I was told that the carpenter who has now left, was screwing the first engineers wife, the engineer found out, and while the carpenter was on the toilet, the engineer fired through the closed door with a shotgun, excuse the pun, but the carpenter shit himself, and un-hurt, came bursting out of the toilet, took a double bladed fire axe from the wall and threw it at the engineer missing on a number of occasions but taking chunks out of the rubberised deck of the passage way.

That engineer is still on board and is still having trouble with his wife, only this time it is a motorman who he has in his sights. The motorman confided in me that he was afraid to go down into the engine room because the engineer might drop something on his head, it is four stories down, and so it wouldn't take a very large object to do a lot of damage. It was on the way to Nauru that they caught the engineer with a shoe off, hitting his wife's hand trying to get her to let go of the hand rail that he had tried to throw her over, and into the ocean. They were both taken ashore in Nauru and I didn't hear any more.

Life at sea can be pretty scary at times, it is man against the elements, but any man who thinks he can go against the elements is a fool. We must always find a way to go with them. 'Go with the flow,' as they say. It's amazing how small a massive 50,000 ton ship can be in a hurricane. I'll tell you a story about a voyage from Adelaide to Japan. We had made good time and were about one day short of the equator, the seas were calm and we looked like getting to Osaka earlier than expected. Murphy's Law states that if something is going to go wrong it will, and at the most in-opportune time.

I was on watch in the engine room when the engine started screaming and missing a beat. The engineer was very quick and had it shut down inside one minute. The thump, thump, of the turning prop shaft came to a stop; the only sound was from an auxiliary generator in the back ground. The 50,000 ton bulk carrier lay helpless. Without way for steerage it lay wallowing like a great whale in the middle of an endless ocean. It was all hands in the engine room, deck crew as well, we had to pull piston while at sea. This was a five cylinder diesel engine and it could run on four cylinders as long as the offending cylinder was disconnected from the crank shaft. The cylinders were wide enough for two people to stand side by side. This was a very dangerous operation, but it had to be done. The piston would swing about the rolling and pitching engine room unless it was kept stable with ropes and pulleys while it was being lifted out. We just had everything out and fastened down, when a message came down from the captain that we were directly in the path of a hurricane, already the seas had started to chop up but not enough to worry such a large ship. The hurricane was about one day away and we still had to put the engine back together, the tension was palpable, but the chief engineer knew his job. One doesn't get to be a chief engineer of such a large ship without many years of experience. Within another half a day we were steaming toward the hurricane, it was too close to run from so we headed for the safest side. I must say as an engineer myself; I was amazed at the knowledge and efficiency displayed by all concerned. From the deck we could see the dark funnel shaped clouds covering the whole horizon, not like a tornado, but wide tapering up into the sky above us. The seas were picking up ahead of the wind, and the air of tension was picking up with it. The waves started to break over the deck and the seamen on the wheel had the ship heading into the increasing sea, and hitting the waves one quarter on. The signal came down to run at half speed, and all unnecessary crew to leave the engine room. We got orders to shut all bulk head doors, and close the steel porthole covers. After a short time we were told to leave the deck level and go up to the next deck. This 50,000 ton ship was rolling and pitching like a cork. When the storm was at its peak, a crewman and I sneaked down to deck level, and opened the steel cover over the double glass porthole, the scene was terrifying, one moment we were looking up at the sky and the next the bow would drop four stories down into a trough with a tremendous shudder that had me worried about how long any ship could take this pounding, then came the water, the four story high wall of water came rushing over the deck and slammed into the bulk head door with a force that shook me almost off my feet and by then I was standing well back. The ship looked like a submarine as it was diving with only the conning tower visible, then just as the water cleared from the deck the ship found another wave to start climbing up, only to get to the top and have it collapse under it, then repeat the whole performance once again.

My thoughts went back to the dockyards in New Zealand where we were replacing rivets in the side of a ship that was in for repair. It was explained to me that in the old days of ship building, rivets were used to join the large steel plates together. But it was a slow and expensive way of ship building. When welding came into popularity, the plates were welded together, so much quicker and cheaper. There was a problem, where the riveted plates could move over each other under stress, the welded plates could not and the weld being the weakest part would crack under strain. I have heard stories of quite large welded ships breaking in half under the strain of very rough seas; their welds had to be inspected regularly. This was a Panamanian registered ship, and I was wondering how often the welds on this ship were inspected.

The Japanese waterside workers, and engineers were amazing, they appeared as ants, their small frames swarming over the ship, each one knowing their job to perfection. We were given shore leave while the engineers repaired the engine. Danska, my Danish friend and I got a lift to Kobe, a nearby city known for its night life. We entered a bar not unlike the bars I saw in America, expensively carpeted with deep red carpets, only larger, with tables and seating on all sides. Danska and I had no sooner sat down than two girls came over and asked to join us. After quite a few drinks and some sensual dancing, my girl asked if she could be my steady girl friend, this was more than I had hoped for so I agreed, that is if she could find me somewhere in Kobe to stay, I felt that it was too far to travel back and forth to Osaka. Lily, 'not her real name, but the name she liked,' introduced me to Mama San, asking if I could stay in her place. Mama San agreed, and told me that I would have to pay rent for the unit and pay for any alcohol we drank from the fridge in the unit. All was settled and I was led out the back to a carpeted stair case, where I was asked to remove my shoes, and then given a robe and some slippers. Lily let us into a very comfortable unit with the keys Mama San had given her. The unit was fitted out with a bath large enough for two, a separate shower, double bed, fully stocked fridge and a toilet so low that you could see that it was definitely made for the shorter Japanese people.

Call me naive, but I actually thought that the money was for the unit and had no idea that Lily was working and got her cut from it as well. Once inside Lily took charge, undressing me slowly and then herself very suggestively, we both entered the shower, and washed each other all over, Lily was well trained in the art of seduction and by the time we entered the warm scented bath, I was like putty in her experienced hands. We made amazing love in the bath, and then I was given the most sensuous massage while lying on the double bed. We stayed in that unit undisturbed for four days, Lily was a pocket Venus and I joked about putting her in my kit bag and taking her home to Australia. I was in love again.

A knock at the door ended the dream, the ship was waiting to sail, and they had informed the authorities, and, armed with directions from Danska, called to take me back to the ship.

Inspirations

*Allowing God to do for us, that which we can't do for ourselves.
Have you ever noticed? That when someone falls or a child is hurt, there is an instant response from within to pick them up, have you noticed that when someone is suffering our heart opens with love toward them. This kindness and love are not energies from outside ourselves, but that which everything is, finding its own level. As we lose fear and allow ourselves to be what we really are, we find ourselves loving without loving, giving without giving, doing without doing. You see, it's just a matter of BE ing. It is in the stillness of BE ing that I know that I AM.
Not my will, but thine be done.*

Living in love with you eternally.

Ronald Russell   Namaste

Chapter Thirteen

Danska and I decided to sign off back in Freemantle, and while there Danska found a newspaper add asking for experienced refrigeration mechanics to work up north in Mount Tom Price, a town where iron ore was mined. I told Danska that I know nothing about refrigeration, but he said he did and he even had the pressure gauges. Danska convinced me that we could pull it off by working together and sharing his equipment. I went into the Freemantle library and looked up as much as I could on refrigeration. I must have learnt too much theory, because when we went for the interview we were informed that there was only one refrigeration job for the first month because the equipment hadn't arrived, I was given the job. Danska was offered a job in the kitchen until the equipment arrived, after much fast talking, and a load of bullshit, we convinced the employment officer to employ Danska in refrigeration and me in the kitchen, as I had much more experience, having just signed off a ship where my job was helping out in the kitchen. I didn't last very long there, I was drinking heavily, and after an extra long thirsty lunch, the head mess man chipped me about being late; I'd had enough of the town and told him what he could do with his fucking kitchen. Back in Freemantle, while drinking at one of the pubs frequented by fishermen, I got into a conversation with a Cray fisherman, his name was Ernie, pretty big bloke, solid build, around forty five or six with a round smiling face. "Wouldn't be looking for a job, would you?" He was looking directly at me, his smile inviting me to answer. "What would I be doing?" I was interested, but nervous. "I've never worked on a Cray fishing boat before, d'ya reckon I could learn?" Ernie slapped me on the back in the friendly manner which says you're ok. "A strapping young bloke like you? No problem, got another deckie to teach you the ropes, and we just do day trips, yeah, I reckon you could learn." I decided to give it a go but was a little anxious when he said we would be leaving in about four hours to drive the three hours up to his place. I had only been back in Fremantle a couple of days and was looking forward to a few more days on the grog. "You'll be staying with me and Elsie my wife, we'll look after your board and tucker, the missus is a bloody good cook, you'll get five percent of the catch on top of that to start, if you can handle it we'll see about giving you a bit more."

Ernie's wife Elsie was quite pleasant and easy going, she had that natural smile that country folk had, "We'll fatten this one up a bit, I've already got dinner ready, just show Ron here to his room and then wash up and come and get some tucker into you."

After a wonderful meal of shepherd's pie, followed by warm apple crumble and cream for dessert, we sat in the lounge and chatted about the state of the world, the weather and how it would affect this week's fishing. Around nine, Ernie suggested we hit the sack as we had to be up at four in the morning. Jamie, Ernie's other deckie was waiting for us at the water's edge, he had a sixteen foot dingy facing out to sea, and it was quite a sea, this part of the coast had no protection, and was open ocean, with large waves crashing in upon the beach, just out past the line of breakers I could see Ernie's thirty five foot boat, it had a wheelhouse at the stern with about twenty five feet of deck in front of it, not very big for these waters I thought. After we had loaded our supplies, Ernie got us to push the dingy out into the waves keeping the bow facing out to sea, Jamie and I were sitting on the middle seat with an oar each and Ernie was standing in the water holding the dingy steady, waiting for a lull in the waves. "When I say go, paddle as if your life depends on it, because it bloody well might." After a couple of large waves passed under us, Ernie pushed the boat and while jumping in over the stern yelled "Go, go, go, don't stop, keep it up, by this time he had an oar in the stern rollick block holding the dingy into the waves, my heart was in my mouth but somehow we made is through the waves to the boat, and after we had climbed aboard, Jamie fixed the dingy to the mooring buoy, the engine was started and we were off heading out into the ocean swell. Ernie had his position worked out by triangulating a couple of land marks from the now distant shore, and the decky's job was to throw the heavy cane pots over the side followed by a rope tied to the top of the pot and fixed at the other end to a float. I think we had sixty pots and when all were over the side we went back to the start and began winching them on board, sounds simple enough, but those pots were about sixty pounds in weight and when you lifted it the weight doubled if you lifted when the boat rose up on a wave. Every now and again Ernie would yell out "White one," and we would run to the back of the wheelhouse as a wall of white water broke over the deck. My back was aching after the first hour, and I wasn't sure If I could make the first trip, I managed to hang on and Ernie said that I had done well considering that I hadn't worked on small fishing boats before. This was the hardest work I had done to this point, and after a month my back went out completely, I ended up in hospital with weights fixed to my waist to stretch my back, the pain was unbearable, and to make matters worse I felt that I had let Ernie down, however when he came to see me, he told me it was quite common in this line of work. I decided not to go back to the Cray boat and headed down to Freemantle to recuperate.

Inspirations

You don't have to know the master
To enjoy the music.
Just to live in harmony
With the universe
Is more than enough.

Living in love with you eternally

Ronald Russell   Namaste

Chapter Fourteen

After about a month of daily drinking, whoring and generally getting into trouble, I felt it was time to move on again, I was getting into fights for seemingly no reason, and the money was almost gone.

I applied to an ad for experienced seamen to take part in a northern turtle expedition. I was accepted along with five other applicants on the condition that we would stay until the completion of the expedition which was three months. We signed a contract to the effect that if we left before three months we would forfeit all our earnings.

The sixty three foot steel vessel with the skipper and six crew, made its way out of Freemantle and up the West Australian coast, towing three, twenty foot dories powered by forty horse power outboards. The high cliffs of Shark Bay came into view and we anchored just off the shallow multicoloured reef which stretched for miles along the coast.

There is something about leaving port on a ship, no matter what size, as the ship leaves the protection of the harbour, there is a realization that you are now as one with the elements, and also under the control of whoever is in charge of the vessel, one doesn't feel able to say 'I've changed my mind, please take me back.'

I found myself in this uncomfortable position of wanting to go home as soon as I found out what the job entailed. I had assumed that we would be searching for turtles and logging their type, whereabouts and numbers, 'I mean the ad said northern turtle expedition.' Our job was to harpoon up to one hundred turtles each day, cut off the breast plate, and about six inches of the shell, measured from the outside edge. Everything else was thrown overboard. This was then boiled until a jelly was formed, the few bones removed, and the jelly packed for a lucrative Asian market. I've never been to war, but I felt like the soldiers in the trenches must have felt when they were told they had to shoot the opposing soldiers because they were there.

Warning ... persons opposed to animal cruelty may want to skip this next paragraph, I'm only writing this because it is important for me to be honest and to own my mistakes and weaknesses.

The hardest part was when the turtles were winched onto the deck; they would be laying there, large sad open eyes, looking into my eyes, asking, is this necessary? They were already dying from the harpoon wounds, so we crushed their skull with an iron bar, and they kept on looking, until they were butchered, and then the sad eyes finally closed in resignation to what is. Those eyes are still looking at me today. I know that saying, 'if only,' is about the past, and of no value, but I can't help thinking, If only I knew then what I know now, and had the courage to say NO to what I knew to be wrong. "We are all one."

I managed to last two of the three months, and saw my first whale shark, the massive silver grey monster surfaced alongside our twenty foot dory and looked to be three times longer, none of us knew it was a whale shark and the movie Jaws had not long been released. For all intents and purposes this was Jaws and we were in its way. The shark took no apparent interest in us and carried on gracefully cruising along the drop off of the reef. There were heaps of other sharks however, some quite large feeding on the turtle meat thrown overboard. I have no doubt they would have eaten us as well if we were careless enough to fall in.

My voyage came to an end off Exmouth Gulf, due to the lack of fresh water to wash in; my hands and legs were covered in painful salt water boils and sores. I could see the houses of the town and some trawlers tied up at a jetty. I lost all resolve to stay and asked the skipper to put me ashore. "You still have one month of your contract to go, you'll lose all of your pay, you don't want to leave now."

I wasn't backing down; I could already feel my feet on the jetty. Just as I was about to speak a monstrous shark flew out of the water as it took one of the turtle carcases. "I'll bloody well swim if I have to;" I actually felt the fear in the pit of my stomach as I imagined myself swimming helplessly among marauding hungry sharks. "I'm off this fucken boat now."

"You know you'll get no money." The skipper wasn't trying real hard to stop me leaving.

I was angry, two painful months welling up. "Who gives a shit about the fucken money, you conned us into his miserable fucking trip from the fucken start." I realise that I was making myself angry, so that I could blame someone else, and avoid the responsibility for where I was at.

"Wisdom is experience learned." If we were to learn by our actions and mistakes, then that would be wisdom, but how often do we feel the pain of our mistakes, in this case, the wanton killing of innocent life, and then overcome it by ignoring the sensations and calling it collateral damage, thus allowing us to commit another similar act in ignorance. This pattern of ignorance followed me throughout my fishing career, justifying all for the illusion of the end result. How often have I destroyed innocent wildlife, and the environment in ignorant justification? Isn't the environment life itself, why do I fool myself into believing that I am separate to all that is, and as a separate entity, can judge and destroy, but now I digress, so back to the story.

I was on the jetty an hour later, nowhere to go nothing to do, feeling free. As I walked carefully along the old wooden jetty, my attention was caught by two men mending nets on the back deck of a large double rig trawler. "How er ya goin?" This came from a short solid fisherman wearing stubby shorts, no shoes or shirt; he pushed his baseball cap to the back of his balding head. "Come off the East Winds did ya?" he asked, pointing to the boat I had just left. "Wouldn't be lookin for a job, would ya?" The gunnels of his boat were level with the jetty; he sauntered over and sat on the edge. "Name's Bert Williams, This here's my son, Robbie," His hairy arm was pointing toward a younger version of himself. "We're working our way around to the Gulf of Carpentaria, chasing Banana prawns; we worked our way up from Freeo, but found we need an extra crew, too bloody hard with only the two of us. Know anything about nets?" He was looking at me expectantly.

I hadn't even said I was looking for work yet, but what did I have to lose? "No, never been on a trawler either, been at sea on merchant ships for a couple of years, and did a few months out of Geraldton on the crays before this."

"How long you on the East Winds?" he asked.

"Two months, supposed to stay three, but I'd had enough."

Bert laughed, "Nets are easy to learn, and anyone who can last two months on the East Winds and has the guts to walk off is welcome on my boat, what do ya reckon, want the Job?" We sailed that afternoon.

The Aloha, was a beautiful trawler, this was its first trip, brand new, with all the mod cons, the best of which, for me at the time, was a hot shower. With a large freezer capacity and extra fuel tanks she could stay at sea for months.

Bert had come from a family of fishermen; his father and his grandfather were both fishermen, along with a couple of brothers. He had been fishing most of his life, and like a lot of men from his generation didn't get a lot of schooling, just the basics, enough to read and write and a bit of maths, His school was the sea, and the environment of which he and the sea were both a part of.

It was a beautiful calm morning, we had just finished cleaning up after a good nights catch, the prawns were in the freezer, and the three of us were idly talking over a cup of tea, the boat was rolling gently, the anchor holding the bow into the gentle swell, I asked Bert how come he became a trawler fisherman, the beautiful calm morning must have made him reminisce, I'll relate the story as best I can.

"I never for one moment thought that I'd be a trawler man, where I come from we didn't even like them, we used to call them fancy pant bastards with their fancy big boats, wouldn't know if the wind was coming from the east or west without their fancy instruments." Bert became thoughtful for a while, sipped his tea, realised he had an audience, and then continued. "probably jealous, we had it pretty rough back when I started, there was this old beach shack where we stored our nets and other gear, grandad built it back in the last century, made mostly of logs, it was rough but solid, it had to be, this was down around Albany on the bottom of the west coast, you get some bloody bad storms coming up from the Antarctic, freezing cold too." Bert shivered at the thought, even though we were in wonderful warm sunlight. "We used to sleep on the nets in the shack. Mum would fix food for me and dad and we'd take off on a horse and cart with an ice box on the back filled with block ice from the ice works in town, I remember thinking that the ice was a waste of time in winter, it was a wonder the fish weren't frozen when we pulled them from the nets. We had a clinker dory when I was a kid and we would put it out to sea through the waves, we had no motor just oars, and it was one hell of a job getting it out past the waves when a sea was running, but when one lives with the sea he learns to read the sea, it's the same for those who live and work in the bush. We would wait for a lull in the waves then go like hell to get the boat out past the breakers. Every once in a while we would stuff up and get swamped, and nets and gear would go everywhere." Bert stopped and thought for a moment, I could see the memories flooding in, and then a smile broke upon his weathered face. "Ha-ha, guess who always got the blame for those stuff ups?"

Robbie who had been listening carefully broke in, "Nothing's changed then, guess who cops it now?"

"Anyhow," Bert wasn't about to be put off. We'd set our nets out past the breakers, and sometimes, depending what we were after we'd go out past the drop off searching for the pelagic fish like tuna. We'd clean them on the beach and pack them on the ice, and when we got a load we'd head off back to town and unload at the markets, next day we'd be at it again. When I was about twenty two I met and married Robbie's mum, and it wasn't too long before Robbie turned up, we were pretty happy and brought ourselves a house and as Robbie grew up he was able to help me with the nets. All went well until about five years ago when Janie, that's Robbie's mum passed away with cancer. I was devastated and lost all interested in life, it was Robbie's idea to sell up everything and build this trawler." He paused for a moment, looked around, and with his arms outstretched said, "And here we are".

The wind had freshened up so we headed into the wheelhouse, and into our bunks down in the forecastle.

We worked our way up the west coast trawling for tiger prawns at night and doing a spot of line fishing during the day. There was so much waste. To sort fifty pound of prawns we would throw five hundred pound of unwanted sea life over the side, most of which had died, but I could justify this. Sometimes great stingrays and sharks, if not killed were badly damaged by the nets.

Life wasn't all peaches and cream on the trawler either, we worked very hard while at sea, sometimes only catching a couple of hours sleep each night, there were so many things to go wrong. It could be quite dangerous as well, having to climb out onto the "Otter" boards at the end of the boom, often in heavy seas which threatened to wash us away if we weren't careful, these boards spread the nets and we had to untangle them after they had flipped over due to a hook up on some submerged object or reef. Sometimes the net would wind itself around the propeller, and had to be removed by diving down and cutting it free, this wasn't always easy, because the wire head and foot ropes would often become tangled around the propeller along with the net. To make matters worse this usually happened at night, and I can tell you that it's very scary having to get into the dark water where not long before dozens of hungry sharks had been following the boat eating the waste product from the previous catch.

Darwin was a great place back in the sixties; everyone seemed to drink to excess and were proud of it. There's even a song that goes 'There've got some bloody good drinkers in the Northern Territory'. I'm afraid I played up pretty badly and got locked up on the second night in town. It's not like I want to get drunk, I just want to have a good time, but lose track of my drinking. Sometimes I catch myself thinking that I might have a problem with alcohol, but I push it aside. How else am I going to enjoy myself? I think that is why I like the sea and the outback, there's no grog on hand all the time, and I don't miss it as long as I don't start. I didn't know it then, but I was on my way to becoming an alcoholic, maybe I already was.

While in Darwin, we heard about unbelievable catches of Banana prawns being caught off the coast of West Irian. It was only a few days steaming from Darwin, so we decided to try our luck. These were new grounds, and only half a dozen trawlers were working them. It's a funny thing about trawler men, when onto a patch of prawns, all friendship goes out the window, and the only thing that counts is the catch, it's like a war zone, but at all other times they can't do enough for each other. We were shown the best way to set our boards and nets; this was a different way of trawling and required the nets to be down to the bottom and back up in minutes, compared to hours while trawling for tigers. We were looking for a solid mark on the sounder, and when we found it we shot our gear away, trawled through the patch, then winched up. We were turning for another pass, but when we saw the nets our mouths fell open in surprise, the cod ends were full to overflowing with golden Banana prawns, completely clean of all trash, just pure prawns. The other boats were watching and were shooting away at the patch as we winched the prawns on board. We had caught more prawns in half an hour than we had caught since my joining the boat. After three days, we were fully loaded and couldn't hold any more prawns, so we headed back to Darwin to unload. While in Darwin we heard that the grounds had been closed to Australian trawlers, something political, so we headed around to the Gulf of Carpentaria. We worked on Tigers around Groote Island, Mornington Island, and Weipa. Of a morning we could see the morning glory building up over the bottom of the gulf and then heading north. This was an atmospheric condition, made of clouds in a huge wave like formation stretching right across the horizon. Recently I have seen pictures of Parra gliders surfing this wave like cloud formation. We needed to refuel so Bert decided to go to Thursday Island, the fuel was cheaper there and they were catching Tigers around the outer islands.

Inspirations

Mind over matter.....If you don't mind, It doesn't matter. "Life on life's terms" Means simply, to accept the cards we are dealt throughout life and play them to the best of our ability. If I don't mind what cards I receive, knowing there are no mistakes in Gods world, then it doesn't matter and I just enjoy this game of life in peace. It is only when I cry over the cards I'm dealt do I lose my peace.

Living in love with you eternally.

Ronald Russell   Namaste

Chapter Fifteen

Thursday Island, (T I) is the central hub of the Torres Straights, and the Aloha was tied up at the main wharf, Bert is still on the boat and Robbie and I are on the veranda of the Grand Hotel overlooking the wharf and the most magnificent view of the surrounding islands and coral reefs. On another table is a large islander playing an acoustic guitar to the beautiful words of 'Old T I' the song starts "Old T I my beautiful home," and finishes with, "The sun is sinking, farewell." The song was being sung by half a dozen men and women, dressed in their daily dress of sarongs, the men in a sarong called a Lava Lava. This is the island as it was, 2 pm T I time and everyone enjoying themselves. A couple of island girls already at our table making light conversation, laughing and smiling that wonderful open pearly white smile unique to these indigenous races. The song meant so much, I felt at home, I felt an openness I hadn't felt before, as there was nothing to hide, they are what they are. There seemed to be no shame in openly telling someone they wanted to be with them.

In the evening, I took a quiet walk with one of the girls along the beach and then back to the boat, as I passed both, couples and individuals, they would smile that same open smile, and say the word 'Yawah,' my friend explained it was a term of greeting, meaning either, hello or goodbye, what a wonderful way to live, so simple. There was a dance that night, down at the Federal hotel, the hotel on the beach where the 'Wongi' tree leans over the sand. The wongi is a wild plum which only grows in the Torres Straights and the Cape. The legend goes that whoever eats this fruit will always return to the Island. I have eaten the fruit, and have left and returned many times; maybe I have one more return in me, who knows?

Everyone was really letting go at the dance, jugs were being filled and emptied almost as quickly, I was aware of my drinking, so didn't get too drunk, I was having the time of my life, having three or four girls asking me to take them home. This had never happened to me before. The whole culture and moral standard was different, not in a bad way but in an open honest way. I had booked a room in the Federal hotel, just in case, and was rewarded with a visit from Sali, The same girl I had been walking with earlier. There was nothing secretive about this visit; apparently she had worked it out with the other girls that she would be with me that night.

All of the trawling lights were shinning onto the back deck of the Aloha, a party was going full swing, it was Saturday night and we were leaving tomorrow. The dance at the Grand hotel had finished and a dozen or more of us had made our way down to the boat, complete with liquid refreshments. I was sitting on the stern railing with a few others, when, out of the corner of my eye I noticed a sudden movement, maybe a startled cry, and a space where a girl had been sitting, I glanced back into the water to catch a glimpse of her being taken quickly away by the fast running tide. The spring tide, running between the islands, can be like a raging river in flood, whirlpools and all. I was over the side before I realised it, the same reflexes which appear out of the blue, I'm instantly doing, without any thought at all. Actually, if I had thought, I probably wouldn't have left the boat; I'm a poor swimmer at the best of times, and in these waters, hopeless. However this was out of my hands, although I didn't know it, and I had the struggling girl in my arms just as we left the circle of light from the Aloha. 'Jesus, what am I doing, Christ, I can't fucking hold her, we're both going to drown' I'm certain there's a shark circling ready to rush in for that last fatal pass, taking my unprotected legs in one massive mouth full. My mind is going at a hundred miles an hour. 'Fuck, she's pushing me under, going to have to punch her to knock her out or something,' Her head is going under, but every time I try to lift her up I go under, I'm getting a mouthful of salt water every time I try. 'Christ I think we're going to die.' Something brushed against my leg, I was kicking out madly, fear rising even more, I kicked again hoping to scare whatever it was away, then a brief moment of clarity as I realised that I was kicking at the girls' flailing legs. The panic had drained whatever energy I had left, I was tired, it didn't seem to matter anymore, I was giving up. I could see the next jetty in the darkness outlined against the backdrop of town lights, the girl was struggling and I was having trouble staying afloat, still taking mouthfuls of salt water. I struggled towards the jetty, I knew if we missed this jetty the next stop was Indonesia. I made a last mighty effort and was rewarded with my arm coming in contact with the ladder on the end of the jetty. It was close to low tide and I could feel the oysters on the ladder cutting grooves into my arm, but I wasn't letting go, my other arm was still around the girl, who had thankfully stopped struggling. I got her to take hold of the ladder and pull herself up out of the water as I pushed from behind, she was safe, but the shock had hit me and realization of what had happened took all of my energy, all I could manage was to hold onto the ladder for grim life. It seemed like ages but was probably only a minute or two before I could pull myself up the ladder.

People from the party were arriving, they hadn't seen the girl go over, but had seen me roll backward off the trawler. My arms were badly cut from the oysters and I was covered in blood, probably looking much worse because of the wet skin. We were taken to the hospital where our wounds were dressed and given antibiotics to prevent infection.

The next morning while I was walking along the esplanade and taking a last look at the island, the girl from the night before 'For the life of me I can't remember her name,' caught up to me, thanking me profusely, saying that she was my girl now, and that her life belonged to me, forever, and that she had to serve me, in any way I wished.

It was like something out of a fairy tale, I was terribly embarrassed and didn't want to hurt her feelings, but I had to let her down gently by explaining, that although it was their custom, it wasn't ours and that I would be leaving later in the day, then agreeing that we would be friends for ever we hugged, she was happy with that and had something to tell her parents, whom I think had told her to offer herself to me.

Bert was having trouble with the engine, and had to order a part to be flown up from Cairns, the closest large city in Queensland. He had been informed that it would arrive on Tuesday, so after we tidied up any last repairs to the nets, we were free to do whatever.

The water was beginning to clear as the tide began to neep, and Sali's brother Dan and I were diving off the reef between T I and Horn Island. Dan had the typical islander build, well muscled, broad chest and around five foot ten in height; his head was covered in tight black curls tinged with reddish blond from years in the salt and sun. Dan had lent me goggles, snorkel and flippers. We were after the Painted crayfish which Dan spears for a living, we were using homemade spears, made with a broom handle shaft, and a two foot long piece of reinforcing rod fitted into a hole drilled into the end, a couple of spear gun rubbers were tied to the other end to propel the spear towards the crayfish which hid in crevasses under the reef.

The dinghy was anchored on top of the reef and we were to swim along the drop off. It was low tide and there was only about three feet of water over the reef but the drop off seemed quite deep and dark to me, probably around thirty feet. All I could think of as I peered down into the depths was how many sharks were down there just waiting for this strange white man to invade their territory. Dan was already almost out of sight, I couldn't make out much more than his flippers as he swam towards the bottom with the ease of one who has been doing this most of his life. There is a talk I give myself when afraid. "If someone else can do it, then there is no reason why I can't as well." I took a deep breath, and 'biting the bullet' as they say, dived down into the darkness after Dan. At least that was the idea, I had only gone about ten feet and could see Dan swimming along the bottom, my ears decided that this was far enough. The pain was unbearable, and as I pulled out of my 'courageous' dive, I realised that I was fighting for breath; my mind went back to the time I was caught in a rip at Tamarama beach a few years ago. I could feel my heart start pumping in fear, as again I looked up at the sun shining on the surface, which seemed so far away. This time though I was wearing flippers and hit the surface in seconds, but I still had my head under the water, breathing through my snorkel, no shark was catching me unprepared.

Dave surfaced close beside me, with, what seemed to me a very large multi-coloured crayfish on the end of his spear, he swam to the dingy and scraped the crayfish off the spear into the dingy using the side of the boat. I had only seen the Red crayfish that I was catching in Western Australia; this was at least three times the size. I told Dave about the trouble I had with my ears and breath, he just smiled "It takes time to get accustomed to the depths, come, let's have a look around the shallow water, look for the feelers, you'll see them waving around." We swam fifty meters and Dave pulled up and pointed to a yellow mushroom coral, called a 'Bommi,' I couldn't see anything other than the bommi, so I shrugged, he pointed again with his spear while moving his free arm to indicate feelers, I finally saw them, waving around as if trying to feel vibrations of some impending threat approaching. Dave signalled for me to follow him and watch. He dived straight towards the feelers, and holding on to the bommi with his left hand to keep from floating upwards, he held the spear directly between the feelers and aimed between the eyes of the Cray. 'Thump' the Cray shuddered and lay still at the end of Dave's spear.

The Cray was dead so Dave removed it from his spear and laid it on the reef. He was signalling with three fingers that there were three more there, and that it was my turn. I copied Dave as best I could, pulled the rubbers down the shaft, and aimed directly between the eyes, my heart was beating heavily with excitement, in my mind I had already speared it, the end of the spear kept wandering off target, then as it was sighted perfectly, I let go of the shaft and the spear sped toward the outside edge of the Cray, I had missed a sitting duck or, Cray in this case. We surfaced, Dave was laughing, "You take too long to shoot, it's gotta be one arm movement, aim and shoot, don't pause to aim." We stayed another hour, and I finally speared my first Cray after another miss, we ended up with seven nice sized Crays for our effort. Dave took them up to the pub where he traded five of them for a carton of beer, he kept one to take home and gave me mine to take to the trawler.

Tuesday, and Bert was fitting the engine part which had arrived this morning on the plane. I was sitting on the veranda of the Grand Hotel with a cold beer, again taking in the wonderful scenery, the hotel was quiet having not long opened, many of the boys had gone out to sea to catch the clear water tide. Much of the island made its living from the sea, either on trawlers, line fishing, or diving for pearl shell, trochus shell, bech de mer, 'sea slug,' and cray fish. Dave was sitting beside me, enjoying the quiet atmosphere, there seemed to be no rushing about, every now and then a pot rattled in the kitchen as it was being moved about in the preparation of some gastronomically engineered delight. I didn't want to go back trawling, I felt that this is where my whole life had led me, it actually had, but I didn't realise it at that time. I just knew that this was the place for this moment. Looking back now, I think. 'What other time do we have, other than this moment?'

I was thinking a lot of this out loud, when, seemingly out of nowhere,

Dave asked, "Why don't you stay here then?" Of course I had been thinking along these lines, but couldn't see how I could stay without letting Bert and Robbie down; they had become great friends, and had helped me so much. I mentioned this to Dave, and, after a few moments he asked. "Maybe I could take your place, I know nets, and I know the grounds in the Straights, I've worked them before." Could this be the answer? "What about your cray fishing?" Dave shrugged. "Crays will be here for years, wouldn't mind a break, the Aloha's a nice boat and I get on well with Bert and Robbie."

Bert wasn't too keen at first, making excuses that he didn't have the cash to pay me off; most of his money went into paying off the trawler. "Send me a cheque when you get paid for the last load, I'm easy." Dave clinched the deal when he told Bert of his knowledge of the grounds around the outer islands. I booked into the Grand on a cheaper, permanent basis, and so began seventeen years of life as an Islander, with small geographical breaks every now and again.

Inspirations

'There are no mistakes in Gods world'
This statement is in black and white, There no shades of grey. We either believe this or we don't. If we do, live by it. If we don't, let it go. Either way, NO BLAME.

Living in love with you eternally.

Ronald Russell   Namaste'

Chapter Sixteen

The next few months were spent getting to know the Island life, doing a lot of fishing and lazing about, and far too much drinking. I'm finding that now that I have more time, I'm drinking much more, but at the moment I can control it to a certain degree, it's not really a problem, any way there are others drinking much more than me. This I know today is the denial of alcoholism. It does my ego wonders walking down the only main street on the island and having island girls calling out as I walk past, "Was dere", and then another saying "Was dere first" meaning that they had slept with me.

Money was becoming short and I hadn't heard from Bert, so I got a job as a casual wharfie unloading the cargo ships that carried supplies to the island. It was here that I met some of the older residents of the Island, all wonderful people; Arthur Ah Mat comes to mind as one who took me under his wing in those early days. When he wasn't working on the wharf he would take his small motor boat out trolling for mackerel along the edges of the reef. I think he was part Malayan, not sure, but he was full of stories about the islands. He would point to a sea bird high in the sky and inform me that this bird would wait for him whenever he came out and show him where the fish were working, it seemed to be true, we followed the bird and we always found fish. Another custom of his which I followed later was that he would always stop for lunch, usually sandwiches prepared by his wife. Arthur would stop and let the boat drift while he calmly ate his lunch, but before he took a bite he would throw half a sandwich over the side to share with the sea gods. I really liked the idea of this ritual; it allowed one to take the time to be grateful for what we were receiving. I asked, "What if we catch nothing;" his reply was to be grateful for the chance to be here.

A big change happened when I got to know Graeme Wayne, a white bloke who lived over on Prince of Wales Island, Graeme was what one might call a character, always getting into trouble of some kind or another, and I found him very likable. He was about the same age as me, much shorter with bandy legs, and a slim build, but that didn't stop him getting into all kinds of trouble with almost everyone on the island, including police. He seemed to be tolerated because he was a character. One of his tricks was to borrow enough to buy a small beer, this would gain him entry into the hotel where he would sit on his beer until he could find what he would call a captain, new comers to the island were his target, then he would tell some of the most fantastic stories about the islands, all the while being shouted by the gullible newcomer, I was one of these gullible newcomers, and I must say he was so good at plying his trade it was a pleasure to be taken down by him, he usually left with a ten dollar note and the promise to show his target some wondrous sight next morning.

Graeme invited me to spend a couple of days with him and his de-facto wife, a pretty island girl about the same age as us. Like I said, Graeme was good at his profession and before I knew it I had purchased two cartons of beer for us and a flagon of wine to give the owner of the dingy that we travelled over to the island in. We partied on that night and the next morning Graeme grabbed an old .303 army rifle, and calling me to follow took off through the bush which came all the way to the beach, there was only about ten yards between the bush and the beach. "We're going to get a feed." He announced as he half jogged along the well worn path that led towards the middle of the island. Prince of Wales 'P O W' is the largest island in the Torres Straits, a diamond shaped island about ten miles by ten miles, or one hundred square miles, and at its closest point is only one mile from T I. Wild pigs and deer populate the island, and it is one of these that Graeme is after. They are not all that easy to get as I was to find out later, but Graeme was an excellent hunter, dressed in only stubby shorts, no shoes, no shirt and no hat, his slim athletic build allowed him to move through the island bush as though he himself was one of the animals he hunted. He stopped dead; we had come about three miles from the beach. Hand up to warn me to stay still; he silently disappeared into the quiet countryside. I strained to see or hear something, nothing, not even Graeme, a slight rustle in the trees above, where the island wind was finally waking up to the new day, silence. Then one shot, bang, no echo, Graeme had hit something, a lot of rushing about then calling me over to where the large bore pig lay, blood seeping from a single wound just behind the ear, what surprised me was that it was at least fifty meters from where I stood, the fact that Graeme managed to get to where he shot the pig in such a short time, and without making any noise, told me this was a very experienced bushman, and not to forget to mention, an excellent shot.

The pig was tied to a pole and then we carried it the three miles back to the beach, where the heart was stabbed and the blood collected in a bucket and mixed with vinegar to stop it congealing; this blood would be mixed a little later with cooked pork to form a most delicious batter.

As is the custom, all of the other six families from this part of the island, came to help and share in the banquet, there were large bowls of rice, and beautifully browned damper, all waiting for the many different dishes being prepared from this one pig. I was to find out later this happens whenever there is a large catch of some sort; it might be that someone has caught a lot of fish or a turtle, sometimes a dugong, or deer, whatever comes in is shared around.

Maybe because I had a hand in supplying the pork, and probably because I supplied the money for a dingy to get a carton of port wine, I was accepted as part of the community. I had a ball, trying to learn island songs, and made a complete fool of myself trying to do island dancing, it was all in good fun, everyone was happy, and I loved Island life.

I slept on a coconut mat in Graeme's place, and late next morning went to explore the front beach, the houses were all made of corrugated iron, nailed to a bush timber frame, most had a veranda like platform out the front where one could sit and contemplate the blue green of the waters between this island and TI. We came across a dozen or more forty gallon drums stacked in a large pile that had been collected by one of the islanders, apparently they get washed ashore here after they have fallen off the large ships that use the straights as a short cut across the top of Australia.

I obtained permission to make a makeshift shelter from these drums, and with a couple of sheets of old roofing iron had myself a home, right on the beach. It only took a trip over to TI to purchase a small kerosene stove and lamp, and the few other basic necessities I needed to be self contained. A hole in the bushes covered with a drum with a hole in the top was my toilet.

I was living there quite happily, taking part in the island life, I'll be forever grateful for the acceptance I received from those islanders. Many comfortable evenings were spent sitting on one or another veranda, singing island songs and doing what they called sit down dances. These dances were performed sitting cross legged, and moving the upper body and arms to imitate scenes from the songs that were sung by all, usually to the beating of a kerosene tin drum. It became a bit of a joke among everyone when the king tides came up and into my 'home' and washed anything on the sandy floor away, they would say that the sea god was looking after me by cleaning my house.

There was another God looking after me as well, and one day he sent a princess to my humble abode, to ask me if she could do my washing. Emily was around eighteen short and with perfect proportion, the beautiful white, wide eyed smile topped by frizzy hair combed in such a way it bushed out even bigger, I really liked this style, and called it her big hair. As far as washing went, I only had three pairs of shorts, having given wearing underwear away ages ago to prevent sweat chafing around the groin. I wore no shoes, shirt or hat. I wanted to please her as she said her mum had sent her to ask, so I handed her two pairs of shorts, I had a shirt but only wore it to dances, no one wore shirts at that time. Emily took the shorts, and came back a few hours later with them washed and folded, she handed them to me shyly with a folded Lava Lava given to me by her father. There was a moment's awkward silence, then Emily, fidgeting with hands that she didn't know where to put, finally came out with what had been the reason for the whole washing thing. "Mum said that I can look after you." She left it at that, and we both stood there in awkward silence as the statement sank in. I thought I knew what this meant but had to be sure. "Does that mean you would live with me, while you look after me?" Emily nodded shyly. It's not as though it was the first time that I had talked to Emily, she only lived two houses away and was at all the dances and feasts, I had thought that she was too young, and even though I fancied her I kept my distance, in case I offended anyone. "There isn't much room here," I was pointing to the drums. Emily was smiling, "Big enough, for us," I wanted this more than anything, but still didn't want to offend anyone; I was a guest on this island and respected their custom. "Are you sure, it will be alright?" This was just my fear talking now, Emily knew I wanted her, and she knew how to handle the situation from here. She turned and while walking away, smilingly said, I'll be here after Ki Ki 'dinner' tonight. So began a love / hate relationship that lasted many years, proving to me that love never dies, and that it's possible to love more than one. For love cannot be divided.

'Love is sufficient unto Love.' Kalhil Gibran

Inspirations

Why are we afraid to be loved? Why do we back off when others pay attention to us? Are we too 'cool' to be seen as vulnerable? Do we realise that we are depriving others the opportunity to love us? Giving and receiving are part of the same action. We all need someone to love; it is the way of love. From now on, I'll allow others to take my hand. Who knows? It may lead to humility.

Living in love with you eternally.

Ronald Russell   Namaste'

Chapter Seventeen

John, my son, was born 12-6-1970. To Emily in the Thursday Island hospital. His birth certificate states, father unknown. This is the sad result of my drinking. I had been living with Emily for over a year. Quite often I would stay over on TI drinking and not come home, sometimes for a couple of days. I would book up my drinks and tell the publican that I would pay him back when I got paid from the wharf job; Bernie, the publican at the Royal hotel, stopped me one day and said that there would be no more money, and that I was in too deep. Bernie suggested that I go to Weipa to work for a few months to earn enough to pay my debt, and have enough to start afresh. He also offered to pay my air fare to Weipa. This happened about nine months before John was born, so I accused Emily of going with someone else, even though she swore black and blue that she hadn't been with anyone, I wasn't putting my name on the birth certificate.

Emily's parents and the other families had got together and built us a house similar to all the others, it was on the land behind my temporary drum home. Emily's father owned a 99 year lease on the land, so we had no worries as far as somewhere to live was concerned. John arrived back home to the cot standing under the shade of the She oak tree in front of the house, and overlooking the white sandy beach and beautiful waters beyond. It was plain for all to see that John was my son. I'm sure that my lack of trust had a damaging effect on our relationship. I had no idea what was involved in being a father, nor did I have any idea about responsibility, I just went about life as though nothing had changed. Emily's father taught me a lot about the ways of the seas and tides. He had a small 12 foot wooden clinker built dingy with a mangrove pole as a mast fixed into the front seat, and an oar as a steering paddle fitted to a rowlock block at the stern. When sailing across to TI he would sail along the POW coast about one mile with an inside tide, then, he would head out into the fast running tide which took him down past the opposite island of TI, by this time he would be out of the rushing tide into the still water, but still two hundred yards off the opposite beach. Once in the calm water he would throw out the anchor and wait until the tide turned and took us into the TI beach. This journey would take fifteen minutes in a motor boat, but took him almost two hours. These islanders lived very much the way they had for centuries, but progress was catching up fast.

My drinking was getting heavier, but not bad enough to worry me too much, the trouble was, that I was bringing the alcohol home and Emily had begun to drink with me. This often led to arguments and fights between us. I suppose I was a practising alcoholic by now, but I couldn't see it. Oh yes, I knew that drinking was a bit of a problem at the moment, but I justified it by thinking that I didn't drink much more than anyone else. Emily was drinking more, and my friends had changed, I didn't mix with those who didn't drink the same as me, so I had no one to compare myself against.

Then came what is known as a geographical; that is, moving to another place where we think it will be better, but we forget that we take ourselves with us. Emily wasn't very keen on the idea, as she had never been away from the island, but I talked her into going with the dream of a lovely cottage in some picturesque setting with a white picket fence, a lovely garden and a chicken pen. The deal was sealed when a cousin from Townsville arrived for a holiday. She was happily living with a white man who had a good job and a lovely home; she said that we could stay with an uncle of Emily's.

Townsville was good to us at first; I got a good job at the local prawn factory as a maintenance fitter, and was earning good money. Emily had family to help with John, and I had found a house for us to rent with the option to buy. I had cut my drinking down by not drinking in the hotel after work, and taking a six pack home to share with Emily. We were saving money to buy the house, and with the money I was making we thought we could have it within one year. We had even arranged the purchase with the owner. I bought an old FJ sedan which we parked in an old corrugated iron shed on the property, no more arguments and life was looking sweet.

Cyclone Althea, one of the biggest cyclones to hit the Queensland coast was upon us. It was Christmas Eve, 1971, and we had a beautifully decorated tree in the lounge, with presents all around the base. The cyclone hit Townsville at 10 am, but well before it arrived we could feel its presence. The local radio station had been giving us the cyclone's position during the night, and was advising us of the correct safety procedures, which we were following as best we could. I had cleaned up any lose items in the yard and taped the windows, in the large bedroom. To create a safe zone, I put our spare mattress under the existing bed, the idea being, that if the worst happened we could climb under the bed, onto the mattress, and be protected by the bed and the mattress above.

The wind was gusting strongly a few hours before the cyclone was due to arrive, and I could see the side wall bowing in about six inches with every gust, I was worried about my poor car in its flimsy shed, but there was nothing I could do. It wasn't too much longer, that the wind stopped gusting and blew with a much stronger steady force. The wall was bowing in much further and I was surprised as to why the window was still intact. Things were starting to look dangerous, so I set Emily and John up under the bed with the portable radio for company, the power having gone off ages ago. As I watched from the lounge room, I could see the wall bowing in almost two feet, the window still holding, Then with an ear shattering screech the corrugated iron roofing sheets started to be ripped from their supports, then, as if by magic the ceiling started to disappear through the opening left by the iron, piece by piece the ceiling was disappearing up into the terrifying storm above. As if being played in harmony with a mighty universe to the tune of chaos, the window blasted into a million shards of glass, followed closely by the whole wall.

I don't know if there is a word to describe the helpless terror that I was feeling at this moment, there was absolutely nothing I could do, I hurried in to join Emily who was curled up on the mattress facing the wall away from the wind with John nestled in her arms, as I climbed under to join them the last few sheets of the ceiling disappeared. We stayed in that position with the rain pouring in until the wind eased. The radio was telling us that the centre was over us and not to venture outside because as it passed the wind would return in the opposite direction just as hard.

Eerie, is the word to describe the calm that existed in the centre of the cyclone. Not a breath of wind, everything was still and quiet, in a way it was even more frightening than the actual wind, knowing that there were winds circling around us at speeds of over 100 miles per hour, ready to strike at any moment. The calm gave us a chance to survey the damage. Almost the entire roof had gone, along with the ceiling and side wall. The bathroom which is supposed to be the safest room, and being on the side hit by the storm was completely demolished, but the trusty old shed housing the car was untouched, amazing, must have been its flexibility.

Reminds me of the story of the palm tree and the oak. The oak was always rubbishing the flimsy palm, continually putting the palm down. "Look how firm and strong I stand, and look at you, blown about by the slightest breeze."

Then one day a cyclone hit the shore where the two trees stood. The wind was very strong and the palm was bending over a long way. "Ha ha ha," laughed the oak tree, "bring it on, I'll bow to no wind," and it stood strong and firm.

The wind wasn't finished and it blew much harder, and by now the palm tree was bent almost to the ground, the oak strengthened itself even more, but because it wouldn't give it had become very brittle and with one large gust, the mighty oak snapped in two and crashed to the ground. After the storm had passed the flexible palm gradually stood back up, undamaged other than a few shredded leaves.

It's better to be like the palm than the oak, makes life so much easier.

The thing now, was to decide where to wait out the next onslaught; we didn't have much time as the wind was already picking up. The next door neighbours were away and their house seemed undamaged, it was high set with a brick wall around the perimeter holding it up. I was all for moving us under this house, as I thought the brick wall would protect us, the wind was blowing steadily now, and pieces of ridge capping were blowing off the tiled roof of the other neighbours' house. Emily refused to go outside, so we settled for the veranda of our house. Even though the veranda was rather flimsy and without a front wall it was away from the wind and still had its roof intact. I had moved the bed and mattresses out there, and because there was no front wall, we could view the storm from a sheltered place. It wasn't long before the whole house was shuddering, and I had visions of the house disappearing leaving only the veranda standing.

The second half of the storm wasn't as terrifying as the first, probably because we had come to accept it and felt that we had survived the worst. There was an extra loud extended crash and the house next door that I wanted to move under collapsed on itself, shifting off the brick wall and onto the ground. As Emily and I watched this unfolding from our flimsy veranda, we realised that we could have been under it, squashed as flat as a pancake.

Althea blew away much more than the house which was uninsured, but our dreams went as well. The house was completely demolished, and we were moved about twenty miles away to temporary accommodation. Life seemed to be much more difficult out here, and there were no houses closer in to town.

The long drive to work tired me, and Emily had no family around. Emily and I started drinking again, and it wasn't long before we were at each other's throats. We finally moved into town and lived with Emily's uncle Sutric and his partner Lucy. They were a very caring and kind couple, who didn't drink, and I shudder to think of the hell Emily and I put them through. Rita was born and we decided to have another go at making it work in our own unit. We were drinking too much and Emily had started to go openly with other men. I couldn't handle this so I moved out to a hotel to live, what a joke, I just drank day and night, I didn't care, but I couldn't leave Emily alone. We would meet in a hotel while she was with one of her men, and because we were both drinking an argument would break out and the next thing I was bashing her boy friend. I never threw the first punch, but I goaded the boy friend into throwing it.

John and Rita were being looked after by Uncle Sutric, I had just had a big fight outside the Allen hotel where a bloke came at me with a large broken beer bottle, he came straight at my face but I ducked and grabbed him by the waist driving him into the wall, I was on top of him trying to pop his eyes out, blood was everywhere, and people were pulling me off him, I was fighting them off, I just wanted to kill him. Gradually some sanity returned and I allowed myself to be pulled off the blood soaked body. "We've got to get you to hospital," one bloke was saying. "I'm o fucking k." I snapped back, shrugging his arm off me. "Better look after that bastard there." I finished, pointing at the blood soaked person being helped to his feet. "No, you have been stabbed, that's your blood on him, take off your shirt." The speaker had the voice of authority so I removed my shirt. To my surprise it was cut almost in half and was soaked in blood. The bloke in charge then took the shirt from me and rolling it into a wad applied pressure to the wound on my back, I hadn't felt a thing; the adrenaline must have deadened the pain. I was admitted to hospital which was diagonally opposite the hotel. He had done a good job on me, I had thirty six stitches outside and sixteen inside and he had scratched my lung but luckily hadn't pierced it.

It wasn't long after this that I was having stomach pains and at times found myself spewing blood. I was living in a pub at the time, in one of the cheap rooms out the back, I wasn't eating very well, and I was drinking every day until closing time, often taking something back to my room. I suspected stomach ulcers, as many of my drinking mates had suffered them. The doctor at the hospital checked me out and then while sitting behind his desk, he clasped his very white hands in front of him. "How much do you drink each week?" He was observing me very seriously. I answered with an amount I thought he would believe. "Not much, about the same as me mates, a few beers after work, maybe a few more at weekends." To tell you the truth I had no Idea how much I drank, and as I wasn't working I was drinking all day. I think the doctor knew I was handling the truth carelessly, and his reply to my answer was. "I think you should give up alcohol for one week, I think it might be affecting your stomach lining, Come back if there's no improvement." As I walked from his surgery I was thinking, what would he know about drinking, probably hasn't had a decent drink in his life, any way any fool knows it's the type of food I'm eating, although I suppose I'll try and stop drinking on an empty stomach, probably should drink more milk as well.

A month or so later, I was back again, same problem, same doctor, but suffering from anxiety as well, nothing seemed to be working out for me, and my head was foggy, I couldn't think properly. He didn't mention drinking but suggested I have a short rest in the mental ward. I reacted to that suggestion, "I'm not mad, I'm just having a hard time with everything since Emily left me." The doctor smiled. "No, I know you aren't mad, this is just to give you a break from life for a bit, until your head clears, you can leave whenever you like."

B-block in Townsville was the mental ward, and because there was nowhere else to put alcoholics some were put in here. I found it quite comfortable for the first three weeks, Vallium to help with the shakes and anxiety, three good meals a day, and a comfortable bed, made up each day. The powers to be never mentioned alcoholism to me, so as far as I was concerned I was here for a rest. There were people getting electric shot treatment, and after this, for a day or two they acted like zombies. I was secretly scared that they would find something wrong with me that needed this treatment. On the floor below were the people with Korsakofs Syndrome, a brain injury caused through alcoholism, one chap used to follow me around the ward until I took him back to his bed, he couldn't find his bed once he left it, and often before I got out of the ward he was following me again. I remember thinking; Thank God I'm not an alcoholic.

After three weeks I was feeling on top of the world, the Vallium were working wonders, stomach pains were gone, 'I knew it was the food.' Time to go out into the world and start a new life. Every day for three more weeks I asked the group I was in if they thought that I was ready to leave, they had to vote on it, and every day they shook their heads. They were my friends for the first three weeks, now they were 'Fucken nut cases, they belong here for life, what would they fucken know.' At the six week mark, I got Emily to lie, saying she was interested in us getting back together, that, along with two friends telling the powers to be that they had work for me, got me out.

Of course I didn't go back to Emily, but I did go out west to Charters towers, where my friends set me up driving bulldozers. I wasn't drinking and with the Vallium seemed to be enjoying life, I loved the open air. All was fine until the bulldozer broke down and my friends told the boss that I was an engineer and could fix it. That was the end of the open air; I ended up stuck in the workshop until I finally left after another spree on the alcohol and a fight with the other mechanic over, who knows what? I was thinking 'Bugger it, I'm going back to the islands, I've had a gutful of this shit.'

It begins with me

For too long have we looked outside. The world changes through me. When I look on the world with fear, I won't see peace. It is only when I recognise myself as pure unconditional love, will I see the world in the same way. While I am fighting in any way, against anything, I am fighting against peace. As I forgive myself, I forgive the world. There is no separation in love.

Living in love with you eternally.

Ronald Russell   Namaste'

Chapter Eighteen

I walked off the jetty where the small ferry that transports the air passengers from Horn Island docks to unload its passengers and freight, and was greeted by Ron Liafoo, a business owner on TI. He is the local baker, and also owns a couple of taxi cabs, as well as quite a bit of property. He asked if I was staying and if I wanted to drive for him. He also had a flat that went along with the job. Everyone on TI seems to use cabs, there is only seven miles of road, but the cabs are always very busy. There are four hotels on the island, three or four hundred yards apart, and cabs are often used to travel between each one.

On a Friday night, it's not unusual to be hired for the whole night by a group who want to party on. They would load the boot up with grog, and then hire me to take them to the back of the island, often I would be included in the party, and many times I had to call the owner to get the cab because I was too drunk. Ron knew the ways of the island, and he had told me about the all night parties, He didn't mind as long as I collected the all night fare and didn't drive after I had been drinking.

Emily's uncle Alfie had a Pearl lugger which he was using for cray diving. I had learnt to dive a bit but wasn't experienced, and because I was family he offered to take me out as crew. He had four dingies with outboards which were towed behind the lugger. I was taught all the tricks of the trade and became a very good diver, Later on I purchased my own dingy fitted with a hookah unit which supplied air to the diver through long hoses, I even had a go at hard hat diving, that's where the diver wears a solid diving helmet, as in pearl diving. While with uncle Alfie we worked the Great Barrier Reef from up near New Guinea almost to Cooktown. We swam day after day week after week; go back to TI for supplies then back out again to continue swimming along the reef.

There were a few close shaves while with uncle Alfie, I'll tell you about a couple of them. I had found a really good bommie, loaded with cray, there must have been at least thirty under it, I was free diving at the time and because we were paid by our individual catch, I wasn't letting on that I had found them, my dingy was anchored above the bommie and I was piling the cray fish up on the sand in a heap, no one knew I was onto them. I had just taken a breath and had speared another cray when a dark shadow blocked the sunlight that was filtering through to the sandy bottom where my stash of cray lay. I glanced up to see a hammer head shark directly above the bommie, and only feet away from my kicking flippers. Instant fear coursed through me, this was no baby, it had to be over twelve feet long, and its beady eyes at each end of its hammer shaped head was looking straight at me, I took hold of the underside of the bommie and pulled myself down, I wasn't using hookah so I didn't have on my weight belt, and my body tended to float upwards. The shark looked as if it was swimming past, then with a sudden movement turned on its own length and headed directly towards me; I had my spear in front of me for protection, not that it would have made any difference. Hammer heads have a curious way of swimming, as they move their tail and body, their head appears to move from side to side, and this large head with its beady eyes on each extremity was slicing through the water and it seemed that there was nothing I could do to stop the advance. The shark must have sensed the cray fish I had piled up on the sand, then when only feet from me made another sharp turn towards the pile of cray fish, with a couple of shakes of is great hammer head it had scattered the cray all over the sandy bottom, my last view before I piled into my dingy was the head and feelers of the cray sticking out of the side of that great mouth.

Rice and flour are the basic supplies on a lugger, all else is supplied by the sea, turtle, dugong, fish, shellfish, and even bird and turtle eggs which we would find on the many sand cays along the reef. It was the end of the day, Sam and I were, diving from the same dingy out of sight of the lugger, darkness was coming upon us, and we were heading back to the lugger when we came across a large green turtle, I jumped onto the turtle and holding it by the flippers got it alongside the dingy, The trick is, as we pull the turtle over the side by the flippers, the dingy goes under water a little and the turtle floats in, then the dingy comes up out of the water again, only this time the turtle was very heavy and got stuck half way in. We couldn't move it at all, and before we knew it the dingy was completely flooded, and because we had a hookah tied to the front seat and a heavy outboard on the stern, the dingy sank to the bottom. We were left treading water with nothing in sight except miles of empty ocean in every direction, the silence was deafening, Sam and I looked at each other, knowing what the other was thinking but afraid to mention it. I was again thinking of sharks, in the fading light, all of the stories come back, like, don't swim early morning or at dusk. It's the movies like 'The Cruel Sea' that do me in, where the survivors of a shipwreck are being picked off one by one by marauding sharks. As a diver I have a respect for sharks, and I see a lot of them while diving, and as long as I'm underwater with them, I'm not afraid, I feel that I have some control. It's only when I'm above water with my legs dangling below that I feel at the mercy of the elements, I suppose that's what trust is, trusting that it will be alright whatever happens, it has been so far in my life.

We could see the earth's curved horizon against the setting sun, then we could make out the silhouette of another dingy and its two occupants heading towards us. We were supposed to be the boat furthest away from the lugger, but they had gone over to a sand cay to collect some turtle eggs and we were directly on their path back to the lugger. I was thinking, 'Somebody up there likes me.'

There aren't many outdoor jobs I won't have a go at, I have a talent which allows me to do almost anything that I have seen done, I suppose I'm the typical Jack of all trades, and master of none. At one stage I was working on the new dam as a mechanic and machinery operator, and then when the new wharf was being built, I was operating the crane putting the pylons in place. I was drinking heavily at this time but was getting away with it; probably because most of my fellow workmates were doing the same. I became friendly with Jeff, one of the carpenters on the wharf job and had taken him diving quite a few times. After work one day, over a few stubbies of beer, Jeff and I made the decision to go south and buy a large enough boat to live on and use as a mother boat for cray divers.

Innisfail found us looking at a thirty five foot marine ply boat, very sturdy, with two bunks in the bow, a nice sized ice box, sounder, half cabin, with a Perkins diesel engine. It wasn't quite what we wanted, but the price was right so we became professional fishermen in our own boat. We did a bit of line fishing around Innisfail then decided to sail to TI.

Working our way up to Cairns, trolling our way along the many reefs for Mackerel and Coral Trout, resting in a sheltered bay at night with a couple of stubbies, life couldn't be better. We sold our catch at Cairns, had a couple of days on the grog then sailed toward Cooktown. The lead lights, showing us the way into Cooktown, were in full view when the motor started to miss, we limped into the wharf just on dark, and decided to leave checking the motor out until morning. Shock of all shocks, inspection revealed that we had somehow got water in the fuel and blown the tips off the fuel injectors, we were stranded in Cooktown and to make matters worse nothing could be done until Monday and it was only Saturday morning.

Two weeks later we were on our way, we had spent most of our spare money on the repairs and fuel for the trip up to TI. We left port with the intention of heading straight to TI and not muck about fishing on the way up. Two days out, and the weather blew up into gale force winds, the seas were at least twice as high as the length of the boat, the steering from the wheel wasn't direct enough with all its pulleys so we fitted a tiller directly into the rudder, this gave us direct control. Jeff hadn't been to sea before we bought this boat, and was quite worried, so was I, but I kept my fear hidden from Jeff in case he panicked. By now the small boat was surfing down the waves like a surfboard down those tremendous waves in Hawaii. Jeff and I were both on the tiller, arms shaking with both, strain and fear, we had to keep the boat on the wave or it would get side on and roll, and being an open deck, it would fill with water and sink. During a small break in the waves, I sent Jeff to fetch the life jackets and a forty ounce bottle of rum we had stored for emergency, I was thinking that if we are going to die it would be silly to leave the rum behind. After donning the life jackets, Jeff and I took turns at swigging rum from the bottle. Talk about rum calming the seas, by the time the bottle was half empty we were surfing down the waves yelling at the top of our voices "Woo Hoo, here's another wave, yippee," all fear completely gone. Our little boat has a top speed of seven knots; we averaged twenty five knots during that experience.

This last little episode brings home to me the fine line between life and death, and how, everything can be going perfect one moment, and gone to the pack in the next. The wind had settled down and we were sailing inside the reef, beautiful calm waters with an odd fish jumping here and there, we were taking turns to have a three hour sleep, and as Jeff didn't know how to plot a course, that job was up to me. I pointed out to Jeff the next light about two hours away and asked him to wake me when we reached it so that I could change to the next course, it was dark now but the light would be very visible. I was sound asleep when

I was thrown out of the bunk onto the deck, as I scrambled out I was calling to Jeff, "What's happened, have we hit something?" Still half asleep I looked up at the light about twenty feet in front of us. We were lying on our side and with each wave I could feel the boat scrape across the reef. "Shit, I told you to wake me when we got to the light, what happened?" Jeff didn't know what to say, he was in shock. "We're not there yet," was all he could say. I looked up at the light again, blinking away just in front of us, and laughed, "I suppose not." As much as I wanted to blame Jeff, I realised he had literally done exactly as I had asked. If I had plotted the next course and asked him to turn before the light we would have missed the reef.

The reef had only about eighteen inches of water over it, the tide had just started to come in and the boat was facing the wrong way, our forty gallon drum of fuel had caused the boat to lay with its side open to the waves breaking into the open boat. Firstly I walked the anchor out to the edge of the reef, the boat was banging on the reef now, and I was worried that the plywood might get a hole or split at the seams. We had to get the fuel drum across to the other side. Water was up to our waist as we stood on the reef trying to make the drum roll to the other side. The boat was filling up quickly now and Jeff was bailing as fast as he could, the only light we had was from the light house above. A larger than normal wave hit the boat which was almost floating now, albeit with a heavy list to the side, and pulled it against the anchor chain holding the bow in position, this resulted in the boat swinging around into the oncoming waves, which allowed us to move the fuel drum to the centre of the boat. We were safe for now, although the boat had developed a leak due to a small opening in one of the seams, the bilge pump would handle that and we could fix the seam on TI.

Inspirations

Within the harmony of the universe there are both failures and successes. We must allow, and accept both to find peace. There are no mountains without valleys.

Living in harmony with you eternally.

Ronald Russell   Namaste'

Chapter Nineteen

The difference between Jeff and me was that this was an experience for him, but for me it was a lifestyle. We had been working the boat for about six months when Jeff decided that he wanted to go back to Sydney, his home town. I bought his half of the boat for $1000, which was much less than it was worth and continued working the crays. I still had my dingy and hookah unit and instead of finding someone to dive with I decided to work by myself.

Bad move, I had progressed to drinking port wine and always had a good supply on board. I had purchased ten cases one day from the grand hotel when they had a special; they were hidden under the bunks in the cabin. I could sell them for four times what I paid for them on the outer islands. It had always been a fantasy of mine, to be running contraband in small planes and speed boats to frontier areas where it was illegal, always staying one very close step ahead of the authorities. I even did seven hours flying in small aircraft with this in mind. I really liked flying but when it came time to fly solo without an instructor in the plane I chickened out, and it would cost too much money to get the experience that I felt I would need.

Anyway I've got ten cartons of plonk on board and I'm out on the reef by myself, working from my dingy and using the hookah. Maybe because I'm a little afraid, I have a few mouths full of plonk to give me that 'Dutch courage' I needed to get started. Once in the water I'm as right as rain, and for a while, just enjoy the wonderful peace of this beautiful underwater wonderland. It's like this most days, being grateful that I am able to spend time in this new and often exciting world away from all human cares.

I put the hookah together myself, and at the time couldn't get hold of a pressure tank, so I used extra long hoses. The safe way to dive is to have a tender in the dingy looking after the hookah and to let me know when the fuel is low so that I can decompress on the way up. All of my life I've cut corners and this is no different. I would start the motor of the hookah up and with a full tank of fuel I would get about two hours of diving in before the motor ran out of fuel. After the motor stopped I could feel the air become harder to suck in, at this stage I would only have two breaths left to surface with. This is a very dangerous practise, especially if I have been working in deeper water. I have lost consciousness on more than one occasion, and I think this may have contributed, along with the alcohol and drugs to the brain damage I had when I finally gave up drinking. I have only recently found out that I had developed a bubble behind my eye which caused scaring of the Macular.

Out of the ten cartons of wine I only sold three, the rest just seemed to disappear. I had no trouble polishing off a flagon of wine while relaxing on the deck by myself watching the sun set over the horizon. When in port I would sell my catch, and proceed to drink, with a lot of help from my friends. A cheap back room at one of the pubs and a girl friend or two was all I needed.

The TI hospital started to become a second home to me, because of my poor diet, the coral cuts on my arms and legs wouldn't heal and often became ulcers, I was on anti-biotic capsules much of the time. Venereal disease was common on the island, but in all of the years there, I never caught it, I put this down to my diet of anti biotics. They didn't work for crabs though, those little insects that get around the genital area, they feel like they have one thousand legs, hang on with one and scratch with the rest.

Timena was my new girlfriend and we had a reasonably good

relationship, as good as could be expected with my drinking, she had been adopted into the Nona family as a child. Her original home, I think, was Saibai island which was up near the New Guinea coast. We had a child on Thursday Island, and we named him Ronald after me. I was hardly at home; either working in Weipa or out cray fishing. Timena was having trouble coping, so the Nona family adopted Ronald. At the time, I was devastated, but secretly knew that I couldn't look after him, I couldn't look after myself. Life on the island was getting too hard with my drinking and all. I knew that drinking was a problem but I didn't know that I was an alcoholic, and I always thought that I only needed to control my drinking and then I would be alright. I would front up to the TI hospital with all kinds of complaints, like the delirium tremens or DT's as we called them, stomach ulcers, headaches that I was sure were Tumours, They would dry me out, feed me, clean me up, and after three weeks I was ready for the world. I actually gave alcohol away for one year on Horn Island using copious amounts of vallium and dope, and then had a drink to celebrate and the next thing I was back in hospital.

One day one of the girls from Horn Island came into the hospital with a present, just a small parcel wrapped in tissue, I couldn't believe my eyes, as I unwrapped the tissue there before me was my false teeth, I hadn't seen them for over a year. They had come across them while raking my yard to make it nice for my return home; I must have spewed them up some time while drunk. Quite often, on release, I would go to another island to live where I wouldn't be tempted to drink in the pubs.

The New Guinea boys hung around in gangs on Horn Island, in those days, and I wasn't the most popular white man, having beaten one of them in a fight. They were out to get me, and one day their chance came. Four or five of them were on the jetty spearing squid and I had to drive my dingy underneath them. The leader saw me coming and raised his spear threateningly, there was no way out, I had to go under him or turn back, I knew that if I turned back I was a goner, I had to hope he was bluffing, so without changing from the slow steady speed I guided my dingy directly under him, my heart was thumping louder than the outboard. As I cleared the jetty I knew he was directly above, and I could literally feel the spear entering my back around my shoulder blades, I don't think I was breathing as I drew away from the jetty, to the jeering calls of "White trash". I had won that one. Although over the next few years I heard that a couple of my white mates disappeared on the way over to TI from Horn Island. The story goes that they were sunk in their dingy by the New Guinea boys bashing their dingy with their larger dingy. It was real frontier stuff in those days. It was nothing to see the police getting bashed after a dance on TI.

One time I was taken in by a friend on one of the back beaches on POW island, he was building his own house on one of the most beautiful beaches in the world, lovely soft white sand, and a view across the beautiful blue green waters to the horizon from where the setting sun would send its magnificent orange rays out across the water directly to our door, it was so peaceful.

My water divining skill was put to good use when I divined a fresh water stream underground where we dug a well, but because it didn't rain for nine months it would get brackish just before the wet season came. I didn't drink too much alcohol there at first, but Doug decided to make his own wine by fermenting canned fruit along with mangoes which were plentiful on the islands, I ended up back in hospital again after that little exercise, and when I came out, stayed in one of Ronnie Liafoo's flats. I was determined not to drink, so when I went to the pub I would drink only Claytons or lemon squash. This plan was working well, and I decided that seeing as I was eating well and my health had picked up, I reasoned that one can of beer wouldn't hurt, it didn't so I had the second. My having only two beers a day made me feel confident that I had beaten my drinking problem, yes it was a battle sometimes, but my willpower was strong, I had finally beaten the grog. About a month had gone by when I found myself down at the wharf on a trawler celebrating a friend's birthday, I had already had my quota of two when a glass of wine was placed in my hand for a toast, I reasoned that as I was now in control I would be able to let go a little just for tonight, I was in hospital before the week was out. I would have had close to a dozen hospitalizations in under two years; I had had enough, so I sold everything I had, and headed back to Townsville. Emily and I had a short fling, but Emily didn't feel the same about me as I felt about her, she kept up with her other boyfriends, and I kept following her around and getting into trouble.

Inspirations

*Love, Kindness, Tollerance and Compassion are the values with which we are created. They do not come from outside, but are the very essence of our being.
If someone falls down and is hurt, or if someone is suffering, We instantly rush to comfort them without thought, we don't call out to the heavens for kindness or compassion, but the love within takes over and we find ourselves instantly helping others in need. This love can be so powerful that a small person can lift a car off an injured child. Others run into burning buildings to save another. We don't decide to give this love; it is what we are,
We are being love, rather than giving love.*

Living in love with you eternally,

Ronald Russell Namaste.

Chapter Twenty

Work was easy to get, but with my drinking, hard to keep, one of the publicans bought a trawler and asked me to skipper it off Townsville working on the tiger prawns, that was good for a couple of months, and I was able to take my son John out for a trip. I was offered a job as a depot manager with the Queensland fish board buying directly from the boats as they docked, but the wharf was only one hundred yards from the pub, so I made the pub my office.

Meanwhile Emily had gone to Darwin, so I followed her there still hoping to get back with her again. I found her in the Don hotel drinking, and was in a fight within the hour. While in Darwin I began to mix with a few of Emily's cousins, and until I got a job, they kept me in grog. A new powerhouse was being built, so I asked the foreman on the job if they wanted any fitters, he studied me for a while then asked "Can you read a tape and use a hammer," I nodded and he went on. "Our work is mainly forming up for the concreters; if you want to have a go, and can handle the job I'll put you on carpenter's rates after a week." There were about ten carpenters on that job and only three of us could read plans, I was a leading hand in a month.

The trouble with working is that I was the one with the money now, and had to keep all my 'cousin brothers' (a sort of defacto relation) in grog. These guys were pretty heavy and it wasn't unusual to see them standing over someone for money, that's how they kept me in grog earlier on. Toby was the ring leader of the gang, about six boys, aged from about nineteen to twenty five. Trouble started when a Swedish guy wouldn't give him some money and a fight started out. The Swedish guy could fight and gave Toby a hiding, but not realising Toby had a gang behind him he took on Toby's challenge to go out the back to the old Tibetan temple and fight again. I knew what would happen and tried to warn the Swede, but he wouldn't listen. The temple was made of large sandstone blocks, walls partly crumbling, and without doors. There was a large room inside where the fight was to be held. I tried again to secretly warn the Swede, but I didn't want to be seen or I would have been in trouble myself. The fight had hardly started when the Swede was tripped, then kicked in the body and then the head, half a dozen blokes were kicking him when I quietly left, I didn't go back to the pub because I knew that this would end up in a mess. I was living under some upturned boats at the time, so I got a flagon at another pub and went home. I didn't go out that night, and the next morning heard that the Swede had been found dead on the side of the road outside the temple; apparently he had dragged himself out there during the night, and died before he could get help. This is the first time I have talked about this incident, and I feel as though I should have had the courage to prevent this unnecessary death. I stayed away from the Don hotel for a few more days, all the while living in fear that I would be accused along with the others. I collected my last pay check on the Friday and got a job on a Barra boat, there were three of us and we worked all the top end rivers netting Barramundi. Later on I heard through the grapevine that two of the gang went to prison.

Crocodiles were everywhere along the banks of these rivers, they would get caught in the nets and have to be freed if possible, sometimes smashing into the dingy with their massive tails. The biggest crocodile we caught was a monstrous seventeen foot six inches long, but it drowned before we could free it. I cut three teeth from this monster and fitted them to a leather strap as a present for John, but he lost them.

The net was caught on something under the water, probably a tree root, I got the skipper to hold the net taught while I swam down to unhook it, the water was very muddy and I couldn't see my hand in front of my face, so I followed the net down hand over hand, it came free fairly easily and the skipper was pulling the net into the boat when something hit my leg with terrific force, there was a swirl in the water and in half a jiffy I was in the boat. The skipper reckons that my feet were in the boat before the rest of me, he said that Jesus had nothing on me, I just rose from the water and ran across the top until my feet were in the boat, I don't know what it was, but my bet is that it was a crock that had taken a fish in the net down to its lair, that's why the net came free so easily.

Low tide, and I've pulled my dingy up onto the mud to clear a large Grouper out of the net, it was high and dry, but they stay alive for days if they can stay damp, it was well over two hundred pounds and it took me about half an hour to free it, I turned to head back to the dingy, only to find that the dingy had drifted off the mud and was floating out to sea. I didn't fancy spending the night on the bank with the crocodiles, so I tried to run after the dingy. Run? No it was impossible to run, the mud was up to my thighs and it was hard enough getting one foot to come free, only to have it sink again up to my thigh. The dingy was getting away and was now over one hundred yards away, I had to swim. I seemed to be swimming for ages, and I could see that I was gaining, but every minute I was in that water there was that much more chance I would be eaten by a shark or crocodile, I just steeled myself and kept swimming. When I finally caught up with the dingy, I put my arms over the side and tried to pull myself in, no hope, I was completely exhausted, and I had to endure another terrifying five minutes with my legs dangling below in the water just waiting for something to remove them from the rest of me. When I finally found the strength to pull my exhausted body into the dingy, I collapsed, lying along the seat for another ten minutes, before summoning the strength to start the outboard and head back to the boat.

Talk about the Wongi calling you back to TI, my stories of the Islands had interested the skipper and he decided to steam over there and have a go at the crays. I worked on the crays with him for a while, using my own boat and dingy, but I was thinking about the kids in Townsville.

Snowy W. had just bought the cargo boat Poseidon, and asked if I would take it to Cairns with him. I jumped at the chance and was on my way within the week. On the way down I cut a corner and put the boat on a reef for a few hours it was tightly wedged on the reef, but luckily the tide was rising, so, with a lot of manoeuvring to and fro, we managed to free it without damage.

Back in Townsville I tried to have a relationship with John and Rita, they would come over to the south side for a Saturday visit, I was too far into myself to make it work. They would play in the park while I would sit in the pub across the road drinking my precious alcohol. One day the police came into the hotel with John and Rita in tow, apparently they had met up with another kid and wandered down to the river mouth where they had climbed into a dingy and drifted out to sea. John was about eight and Rita five or six, someone had seen them drifting out to sea and called the police. I was terribly embarrassed that this could have happened, the embarrassment turned to anger. I couldn't accept responsibility; I had to blame them and scolded them severely. No, I didn't think that they might have been killed, I didn't even think to thank the police officers who were actually looking embarrassed at my reaction, I just thought about myself and how they could have done this to me. When I got the two frightened children home, I let uncle Sutric know how bad he was at bringing up children.

By now I had become unemployable, and was sleeping wherever I could find shelter, under fig trees, under bridges, sometimes when it was raining I would climb over the wall of a locked toilet block, badly cutting my hands on the broken glass that was concreted to the top of the wall to prevent climbing. I would visit Saint Vinnie's and the Salvo's for a loaf of bread and sometimes a tin of spaghetti or baked beans, I was in a bad way.

The police were locking me up every other night; I can still see that 'drunk' tank where they would throw us poor unfortunates. Yellow concrete floor, stainless toilet in the middle of the back wall, tin cup next to it to get water from the pan to drink, no bed or bedding, sometimes fifteen drunks thrown in there when there was only room for ten. They reckon if you got seven nights straight the judge would give you three months in jail to dry out, couple of times I got close. We weren't doing anyone any harm, I don't know why they bothered to pick us up, it only cost them paper work.

It wasn't too painful living in the parks and sleeping under bridges and the like, because I had given up giving up alcohol, it was too hard and painful to give up, so I decided to stay drunk, I became a twenty four seven drinker, and because I wasn't working, had to drink whatever was available. People who live on the streets live by the code of looking after each other; at least they did in those days. Whoever got some money would supply the rest of us, and so it went each taking our turn. There wasn't always enough to drink so we would fortify our wine with metholated spirits, it took a bit of getting used to, but it had a kick and was cheap. We would sleep wherever we put our heads, and on two occasions one of us didn't wake up, life had become too hard for them.

My memory of that time, maybe a couple of years, became pretty muddled, possibly, because I spent much of it in a black out, a blackout is when you don't remember what you did or where you were the night before, and the only way you know is when someone tells you, and I'm here to say that it's usually very embarrassing.

When you are drinking all of the time, there is no night before, day and night just run to each other. I can't remember showering or owning a tooth brush, dunking my head in a fountain or under a tap in the park was good enough, I didn't own a towel and a blanket was impossible to keep for very long.

Somehow I ended back on Thursday Island, I have no idea how, and my brain was pretty fried. I can see myself building a shack on Horn Island, out near the airport. I was building on a concrete slab left over from the war when it was an army base. A friend who lived up on a hill not far from where I was had quite a few marihuana plants growing, and gave me some to grow. The plan was to give up alcohol using vallium and dope to recover.

Talk about a fried brain before, after one year on this regime with a small bust in the middle which again had me hospitalised, my brain was completely cooked. I have a faint recollection of me sitting in front of a huge fire with a flagon of port wine in my hand, then nothing, until I became aware that I was in hospital again.

It was a couple of days later that the doctor in charge came to me saying that this isn't a motel and that I couldn't keep running into hospital every time I needed help. I was sort of expecting that, I was surprised that they let me go for so long. All I could do was to ask him what else I could do. "Well, there is nothing we can do for you here, but there is a place in Brisbane where you might find help." I was thinking, Brisbane was ok years ago, and it looks like I can't stay here. "Ok,' I was resigned to go with whatever. "How do I get there?" "You can stay here until you are well enough to travel, and in the meantime we can arrange transport and accommodation for you once you get there." The doctor turned and smiled as he left, I think he was happy that I had agreed to go away for help, he had known me for a long time and he always remembered my name whenever we met.

It was three weeks before I left TI by plane, I really had nothing to take with me, I had decided not to go back to my shack, I just wanted out of there, a friend loaned me a shirt, and another, a suitcase. The trouble with the suitcase was that it was leather and with nothing inside, lay flat, so I filled it up with scrunched newspaper to make it look full. I had a red thong and a blue thong on my feet that I had picked up on the beach a week or two before entering hospital, I went straight to the airport from the hospital, in my wallet was a ten dollar note some mates had collected for me. I don't remember getting on the plane or off, my head felt like nothing worked, everything was fuzzy, might have been the tablets, but probably a mixture of fried brain and tablets.

Inspirations

We walk by them every day, sit next to them in public transport, but we don't see them, and when we do see them we are afraid. You see they are not like us, not well dressed, possibly unwashed, we don't see them laughing and joking with their friends. There is something sad about this picture, maybe, just maybe, we could find a little courage, just a little time for a friendly word; lend a compassionate ear, or kindly smile, sometimes that is enough. No, not for them, but for us to realise the power of love within. You see, we really are one.

Living in love with you eternally.

Ronald Russell Namaste

Chapter Twenty One

They have dressed me in blue and white striped pyjamas, me nerves are shot to pieces, just spewed up green shit, nothing else there, shakin like hell, need someone to roll a smoke for me, bloody scary place. I remember my first look from outside, 'Biala,' Drug and Alcohol Rehabilitation Unit. Big high building, all bricks and windows, I'm gonna spend the rest of my life here I'm thinking. Just up the road, big yella 'XXXX' callin me in, only got ten dollars me mates collected for my trip here, better buy tobacco, might just get one stubby of XXXX.......... Shit no money left, had four stubbies, hope they take me in with the grog in me.

They allowed me in, only because I had come all the way from Thursday Island. They took all of my tablets and told me that I would have to wait until tomorrow to be prescribed more, hence the shaking. Slowly, ever so slowly, I came good; I could roll a smoke without spilling too much tobacco, and could keep the food on my fork for two out of three forks full. There was nothing to do, "Fuck, how am I going to stay here forever, can't even bloody read, me friggen head won't stop still, like a can of friggen worms all wriggling around in my brain, shit, that's what I reckon shit, bloody shit. It was better when I had my own tablets; I could take 'em when I needed 'em. Bullshit, that's what I reckon, they're all bullshit. No one can live here forever, friggen hell.

No one had suggested that I would be there forever, that was all from my head, actually the average stay was three weeks, this was a detox unit and after you are well enough they ship you out to a proper rehab, or home, if that's what you want.

After three or four weeks, they came to me with photos of farmland, with a cow standing by a dam, trees everywhere. "This is Wacol," the social worker was telling me. "It's a rehab where you can stay until you get well." I have a photo of me standing outside of the unit, stubby shorts, as skinny as a rake, extra long arms probably accentuated by the very thin build, and grey hair. I was only forty two years old and my hair was at least sixty percent grey, mustn't be many vitamins in grog.

It's strange this disease of alcoholism, they call it the disease of denial. Even though I had been through all those years of uncontrolled drinking, and combined with the fact that I was in an alcohol rehab and had been diagnosed as suffering from chronic alcoholism, I didn't believe that I was a real alcoholic. Yes, I had a drinking problem, but my mind was telling me that with education and a spell away from alcohol that I would be able to have that magic two drinks, or a glass of wine with a meal. The fact that I had never been able to do that before wasn't an issue, this time it would be different. I'm very lucky that I had hit a rock bottom, although I was to hit another, the rock bottom of all rock bottoms, and without drinking, two years later. I'm told that alcohol is not the problem, only a symptom, the problem is within me. This became increasingly evident the further I got from my last drink, my head started to clear a little and with the clearing came the thoughts, millions of them, thoughts about the past, thoughts about the future, never a solution, just thoughts over and over. Many times I wanted to drink to end the thoughts, and go back to the fuzz where there are no thoughts, vallium helped a little, but to stop the thoughts I would have to wipe myself out with the tablets. In reality the tablets were not much different to the alcohol.

Time to leave...I had learned to look after myself a little, and learned a bit of responsibility, like making my bed each morning, sweeping and mopping the floor, washing up after meals, and one very important one.... mixing with others without alcohol, something I could never do even as a teenager. I still needed a lot more practise in this area, but I was improving. Group therapy helped a great deal, especially in the areas of trust and mixing with others, and one on one, or face to face counselling helped me get through many personal issues, but leaving? The fear welled up inside. 'Leave, I can't fucken leave, where do I go, and what do I do?' My mind was off again at a hundred miles an hour. 'Bullshit, they can't just throw me out on the street....Can they? Shit, if I go out there I'll have to drink, you can't live outside a rehab and not drink, every fucken one drinks, how do you find a girl, how do you get a job, how do you relax? The whole fucken world drinks.' I had a sleave of valium which I had scored off one of the inmates who had brought them in off the street. Two of these calmed me down and after an hour with Vimla, the psychologist, we arrived at a plan to set me up in a half way house. Vimla was from India, Ceylon, or one of those countries over there, she had dark skin and the most pleasant welcoming smile, she had a red dot between her eyes just above her nose where the third eye is supposed to be, I felt that I could tell her anything, and I pretty well did, a year later Vimla was to play a big part in my recovery.

There were twelve rooms in the half way house, situated in Ascot, one of the more eloquent leafy suburbs in Brisbane, and from the outside there seemed to be nothing special about the house, it was just a very large home in an expensive suburb. I don't know if it's true but I was told that Mr Arnott from Arnott's biscuits owned the house and let the house at a very minimal rental as part of his community spirit. Inside there was upstairs and down stairs, a very large kitchen backed onto a wonderful lounge / dining room complete with pool table and TV.

After being introduced all round, I was shown the roster with all our household jobs on it. One of the clients had been voted in as a manager by the other eleven clients. And it was his job to see to the general running of the house. Every Monday evening Lyn, a counsellor from Biala would sit with us in a meeting, there we could air our grievances, and plan the week ahead. In effect the house was being run by us, the clients. This was very empowering, and went a long way to getting us ready to leave when the time came, around two years, give or take a bit.

I made a couple of close friends while in the house, one, Tony, a good bit younger than me had a drug problem and had tried to end it by jumping in front of a train, He had some horrific scars to his torso, arms and legs, and I suppose many more mental ones, but he was very positive, and having been here a year already, was very good for me. We would walk for at least two hours each day, sometimes into the hospital where we attended counselling sessions at 'Pav 4', a detox unit, Tony was also into new age stuff, so we would go to the relaxation centre where we could borrow new age tapes, and every now and then sit in on a talk by some spiritual guru. This was all new and interesting to me, but I was having a lot of trouble remembering anything, Oh, I could remember all of the old stuff that I didn't want to remember, but I was having trouble with what I called my fuzzy brain, my short term memory was shot to pieces. My doctor had diagnosed me as being manic depressive, I think they call it Bi-Polar these days, and I was already on anxiety medication. I was referred to the royal Brisbane hospital, where I was given a brain, or CAT scan. I asked the technician what he found and he laughingly said, nothing, meaning no brain. I'm not too sure of the results, but I know there was frontal lobe damage, and I was told it could improve in time. I was prescribed more tablets and placed on a disability pension. When I left Wacol, Vimla, told me that I was welcome to come back to the rehab if life got too hard, she said that she would rather have me come in sober rather than drunk. She told me that many who leave the rehab are back after a couple of months having used alcohol or drugs when life got too hard, my mind went instantly back to my hospitalisations in TI where I had done that exact same thing.

My first visit back was after three months, I wasn't sleeping and I kept thinking that it was all too hard, I felt that if I could get drunk then I would get some sleep, and sober up again later on. The main thing stopping me was that I would have to leave the halfway house, and I would have to go through detox again. I took the rehab option. I was about one year sober when I ended back in Wacol again, similar story, but after three weeks of therapy I was ok again. Today I know that behind all of these visits to the TI hospital and the rehab was a search for love, not sexual love, but the love a mother has for her child, spiritual love, there was a hole inside of me that couldn't be filled. My heart was aching and my spirit lost, alcohol for a while had filled this hole, it had been my friend, but it had let me down in the end. The nurses, counsellors and psychologists, were my substitute for this love, and went a long way towards filling this hole, be it only temporarily.

Inspirations

If we are honest with ourselves, we find that very few of us want to hurt others. The inner us is loving, kind and compassionate. It is only when fear drops its veil over us that we lose the awareness of love, We become whatever energy we are using, If we are using hatred jealousy or anger to fight the fear, then we become that energy, every cell joins forces to fight the fear, and is infected with the same hurtful energies. It is when we realise the existence of the deep eternal within, which does not fight, or strive for its existence that we become aware of the futility in fighting something outside of this love. I love the saying "Fear knocked, Love answered, No one was there."
Allow Love

Living in eternal love with you

Ronald Russell   Namaste'

Chapter Twenty Two

Tony had got hold of the book 'Drawing from the right side of the brain,' and after a month's practise, showed me his before and after drawings. I was totally flabbergasted, from an ugly stick figure; he had progressed to a life like portrait of a famous actor. I had the book the next day. Hopeless, is the word I would use as far as my ability to draw went, but as with Tony, after a month my drawings improved out of sight. There were more advantages other than drawing for me, this was actually Zen drawing, and I suffered horrific headaches from the exercises involved in getting my right brain to work. I became interested in Zen Buddhism after this. I also think that it helped with my memory loss. I became addicted to drawing and painting, doing a portrait painting class with Piere Tourene, a recognised artist of the time, I even had some works in art shows where I sold a couple of my paintings. There was one painting that I wish I had kept, it was of a sad, lonely man dressed in a large dark overcoat, standing on a small wharf beside a ships bollard, a bottle in a brown paper bag in his left hand, the night was dark and overcast, and the motionless river reflected the lights of the tall city buildings opposite, its many multicoloured ripples, a contrast to the dark night, and a single, lonely street lamp seemed to be the only company he had. I had captured the essence of myself in a self portrait of my life. The loneliness one feels in a big city among millions of people is to me, much deeper, and completely different to the aloneness one experiences in the bush or at sea, and carries with it a heartfelt sadness that could only be called a soul sickness.

It was this soul sickness that brought me to my final rock bottom. I had just prepared a cut lunch to take to a new job I had arranged to start. Last Friday I had applied for this job to retrain me in the finer points of my trade; this was arranged through a government rehabilitation program. After I had been accepted, I was shown around the workshop, I hadn't really been in a workshop for over twenty years, fear was walking with me through that workshop. As I was shown the lathe I was supposed to work, my mind kept telling me, you've got to be joking, there's no way you are going be able to operate that machine, and as I observed the other workers confidently doing their work I knew my mind was right, every bit of knowledge that I might have had in this area had left me, and the last straw was the time clock. I was introduced to the time clock, which to most, was an innocent piece of machinery which sat quietly waiting for an employee to place his work time card in a slot, pull its handle, and the time that the employee started work would be permanently imprinted on the card. This wasn't how I saw it; I saw this as an evil machine that took away our freedom, something that controlled our lives by time. I had spent too much time on the islands living life without clocks, living with only the sun, moon and tides as my time piece. To have to come here and start at precisely 7.30 am, and have that time recorded by a machine, and no matter how hard, or quickly I worked, my pay would be deducted according to this time machine, no thank you. 'Drunk?' Maybe I might have handled it for a short while, but I was close to two years sober now and as anxious as hell.

Time to leave for the job, I placed my lunch into the lunch box an as I walked towards the door my stomach started doing flip flops, I had been worried about starting work since Friday, and had very little sleep. It was the time clock that got to me, as I walked to the door I had a vision of that time clock just waiting there for me, its card with my name printed in bold letters across the top, my stomach heaved and I vomited over the carpeted floor, My stomach cramped and I vomited again. I knew that I couldn't go to work today. Then I found a sort of courage, and found myself making the decision that no matter what, I would never work in a workshop like that again, and with that thought, that decision, the fear and anxiety left me.

My doctor was studying me from his side of the desk. He was asking if I had experienced this before. "I can't remember vomiting before, although sometimes when I am experiencing extreme danger my stomach would do flip flops." "Hmmm," the doctor had his hand to his chin in the recognised thinking pose. "What about similar work environments, like workshops, do you like your trade?" I was shaking my head "I don't mind my trade too much, but I have always felt uncomfortable in the workshop environment." The doctor was writing on his pad "I'm pretty sure you are suffering from Ergophobia." My mind reacted instantly, not another label "Ok, what's Ergophobia?" "It's fear or aversion to work," he handed me a script "These should help, just take two when you need them." I was thinking, more friggen tablets. It seems that whenever I go to the doctor I get more tablets.

Lyn the counsellor was asking if I had thought about what I would do when I left the house. 'Shit, more stress,' I hadn't even thought about leaving the house. My mind was off again. 'I don't need this shit right now, fuck, I haven't been here much more than a fucken year yet, and I've got all these bloody tablets to take just to keep me going, might as well fucking be dead, who would give a shit any way, I've got no fucken family anyway, shit, bloody shit, shit'.

I looked down at the handful of tablets that I was about to take 'I've had enough, I don't want this shit anymore, I'm not free', and with that thought I threw the handful of tablets into the toilet and flushed it, then I went to my room, collected all of the bottles and packets and emptied every tablet down the toilet. 'That's that,' I said to myself.

'God works in mysterious ways.' I was in the city looking for the Circle Bookshop, where I had been told I could find some good new age books, I walked past a doorway where a little wizened old man was taking books from a multitude of boxes scattered around the floor and placing them on partly filled bookshelves, thinking he might know where the Circle Bookshop was I wondered in, I could see that the shop wasn't open, but the old man came close and looked up from his five foot nothing height "Can I be of any help to you?" he was very polite with a slight accent. My first thought said Jewish, although I had no idea what Jewish looked or sounded like. "I was after the Circle Book shop; it's supposed to be around here somewhere." I was studying the half empty shelves for something to my taste. "Is there anything in particular you are looking for, I'm not open until next week, but I may be of some help, although I don't know where the bookshop you are looking for is." When I came into town I wasn't looking for anything in particular, but another friend in the house was studying and using the 'I Ching' and had been telling me how it was helping him, so out of the blue I asked "you wouldn't have the 'I Ching' would you? The following, is so far out there, I can hardly believe it myself. He smiled as though he knew before hand what I was going to ask for, and walking, directly over to one of the shelves, stood on his toes to pull down a book from the dozens that were on that shelf, he didn't hesitate at all, he knew exactly where the book was. 'When the student is ready the teacher appears'. He was holding it lovingly in his hands, turning it over and carefully wiping a speck of dust off the cover. "This is the 'I Ching', It is my own personal copy, I'm afraid it has some of my notes in the margins, but that shouldn't worry you, he again reached up and came down with a book called the 'Tao Te Ching', and after handing this to me and without saying a word, reached again and came down with another book, "I know the author of this personally, I'm sure you will get something from it." As he handed me the third book I noticed that it was about Tai Chi, The name was 'Embrace Tiger Return Mountain'. How did he know I was interested in Tai Chi, I had been trying to practise it daily since an instructor had taught me some basic moves at my last stint in rehab. This book, although small, taught me the philosophy of Tai Chi. I really wanted these books but I was worried about the cost and how I was to pay for them. As though the little 'Jewish' man could read my mind he put one hand under my hand holding the books and his other on the top. He was smiling as he pushed the books towards me speaking in that same quiet, polite voice. "No, you don't have to pay for them, they are yours, I have been waiting for someone to give these to, and here you are." I knew that these were very special books, but I was out of my depth, and I didn't know how to accept them. "But won't you need them for reference?" He smiled again "No, I won't need these again. I've had these for nearly twenty years; I have crossed the great water, and moved on, now it is your turn." I didn't understand then, but today I know he meant enlightenment. As I thanked him and turned to leave he called me back "Here you will need these,' He handed me a small leather container with a piece of red felt and some Chinese coins with square holes in them. "The directions are in the I Ching, make it a ritual, find a special place where you can consult the book, and use this place like a shrine, and remember, this book will talk to you, you don't even have to open it, sit quietly with it in your hands and it will speak to you. I know this all sounds farfetched, but it happened exactly as I have described.

All this sounds like I was in a good place, and I was on that day, but as the book of changes states, "Everything changes but change itself." I was soon in a dark depression again, every day wanting to die and end it all, since stopping the tablets my head was going at a hundred miles an hour, but I was determined not to go to the doctor for more pills, I had a couple of joints but that seemed to make it worse. I was desperately trying to understand the I Ching, casting coins half a dozen times each day, and to the best of my ability I was practising Tai Chi and reading Embrace Tiger Return Mountain.

I was on a search for God, or what I thought to be God. That, whatever it was, that had come to my aid so many times in the years past, I knew that it must be there, but where, the I Ching was taking me to the great water, but I didn't have what it takes to cross over. This depressed me even more, until one day I had decided I've had enough. I had thought about drinking to get away from it all, I was thinking that there must be a chemical missing in my brain that had been destroyed and replaced by alcohol, and that my brain couldn't work without alcohol, but I knew that drinking wouldn't work either. I was in my little 8 foot by 10 foot room, when I realised that I was on the second floor, I looked out of the window at the concrete path below, climbing out onto the ledge I could see that if I dived head first onto the concrete path all of my worries would be over, then the thought occurred to me that if I missed the narrow path I would probably end up breaking my neck and have to spend the rest of my life in a wheel chair. Anyway I didn't really want to die; I just wanted this shit to end. I climbed back inside and sat back on my bed, my back against the wall and my feet stretched out in front.

Inspirations

In the darkest night we find the brightest light. There is always a gift. No matter dark life becomes, how long the hell seems to last. Know and trust that this too will pass, and as it does the gift will be revealed. Search for the gift in your sadness, There is always a gift.

Living in love with you eternally.

Ronald Russell   Namaste

Chapter Twenty Three

I was playing mind games, looking for God, still sitting in the same place on my bed, I would look in front of me and around the corner in my mind, then behind, it was as though God was playing hide and seek, wherever I looked, He wasn't, I must have been playing this game for fifteen or twenty minutes, when I gave up I just said "Fuck this I give up." Almost as soon as I said this my mind was transported to another plane. It was as though at one moment I was here in bed, and the next I was on another plane altogether, parallel but above, I wasn't there as me but as some kind of energy, almost like the dots you see if you close your eyes after being in bright sunlight, or stars in a milky way that went on to eternity. Everything seemed to be in chaos but it was ordered chaos, all was in harmony nothing banged into anything else. This is probably impossible to describe even to myself, I have a friend Rebecca who calls it the unwordable, which I'll borrow for a while. It was as though I had become the universe, or maybe the universe became me, all knowledge existed there, sort of like letters before they form words, and I knew that this knowledge was available to everyone as long as they allowed themselves to be in tune with this chaotic but harmonious universe, I remember thinking afterwards that this is where all the inventions come from, The scene, if that's what you would call it, changed, or sort of changed to a nothingness, which seemed everywhere, and I wasn't there but I was there, but as nothing, I WAS the nothingness, and at the same time I WAS the everywhere, and at that moment I KNEW that I / this was what people call God, Love, Peace. As this experience passed I felt an overpowering feeling of joy, and happiness, something like a voice said "It will be alright." I stood and walked from my room, I felt clean, there were a couple of people in the lounge and they didn't notice anything, but I did, it was as though I saw them for the first time, and as I went outside, it was the same with the trees, they were different, as though I had on some special glasses, everything looked as though it had just been washed by a cleansing shower. Then I was on the street, I wasn't separate any longer, I felt love, I was love, my heart was singing, I looked at the sky, and the thought came to me, maybe I'm Jesus, maybe I've finally come to earth. With that thought I felt fear; I pictured someone sitting in an insane asylum with a permanent smile saying that they were God, and I knew that could easily be me. The love and joy was almost overpowering, I knew that what I was experiencing was true, I knew that I had crossed the great water, but I didn't know how to handle it. Maybe I did belong in an insane asylum.

Vimla, the psychologist from the rehab came to mind with her third eye dot on her forehead, she would understand. Vimla was smiling while I told my story, especially when I mentioned that maybe I belonged across the road in Woolston park mental asylum. She explained that it is what Psychologists call a psychic change, and in Alcoholics Anonymous it is called a spiritual experience, and that it is often brought on by trauma, well I had definitely been through some trauma. Vimla also suggested that I stay in the rehab until things settled down; she also suggested that I don't tell anyone about this.

Other strange experiences began happening to me, and I'm so glad I contacted Vimla and not a psychiatrist, who might have given me drugs. Today I see this spiritual experience as a psychic event and what is needed in these events is support and validation, we are not mad, even though we and those around us think we are. We need to have our experience validated. That is much easier today; with thousands maybe millions of people around the world having psychic episodes, and books are being written about these every day. I see these events as a natural healing cycle, and if let run their course with support and validation the mind will heal itself. Not back to where it was before the event, but to a whole new understanding of life as it is.

My body is vibrating, maybe not vibrating, murmuring, everything around me is vibrating, shimmering, my feet aren't touching the ground, nothing is solid, I'm sure that I can walk through that brick wall, better not, someone might see me, shit, this can't be real, fuck I don't like this, it's getting worse, that bloke in group therapy yesterday, bloody hell, he had that pain in the side of his head for years, I could feel it while he was talking, somehow I've caught the bloody thing, and he just told us in group that he has lost it, first time in three years, shit, and I knew what everyone's thoughts were. Vimla must know a bloody lot, I'd have put me away long ago, and she just smiles and says "It will be all right." There are those words again, I wonder if this ends? Christ what now, It's getting dark, but its only lunch time, no it's not dark, I'm seeing dark, like a day dream, am I dreaming? Don't think so, I'm pretty sure I'm awake, I'm feeling scared, it's like I'm standing at the North Pole or somewhere, it's dark here where I'm standing, all sharp jagged chunks of ice all around, not really ice, just like ice or something, moving, bumping, crashing in the dark reaching all of the way to the orange horizon away in the distance, I'm safe here, but I know I have to cross the ice to the horizon, fear, unbelievable fear, fear in every cell, that voice again, "It will be all right" I know that I have to trust that voice, every part of my being wants to cross that dark threatening distance. Psalm 23 comes to mind. "Even though I walk through the valley of the shadow of death, I will fear no evil." I've got it, it's the 'great water', I haven't crossed the 'great water', I'm here, now, all ready to cross, I'm on the brink, the fear, the darkest fear, the unwordable fear, I'm paralysed, what's wrong? I can't move, shit maybe this is death, if I cross I'll be dead, this must be God giving me the choice to live or die. I turned to look behind me, maybe there was a better way, but what was darkness and jagged ice was the wall of the rehab office, quickly I turned back, it was gone. A dark mist seemed to be settling over me, it permeated every cell of my body, I was overcome with a sadness of the like I've never before experienced, a grey, dark sadness; I knew that I had lost something so very special. This darkness didn't last, it was more a realization, I knew at my deepest depths that I had found God, not a God of all that is, but a God that IS all that is, a God that in all reality is nothing more than Love, unconditional Love. I hadn't lost any of that first major experience at all; I have never lost the knowledge that I and God alike are Love. I have never forgotten the oneness which, is to me today "Living in Love". What I did forget was that the oneness I had experienced was within, and because I wanted more, because I wanted to cross the 'great water,' I went on a search which lasted years. I found myself craving for the experiences that I had missed through fear, I knew that fear wasn't real and if only I could get to the vibrating stage again I would overcome the fear and walk through those brick walls, or cross the 'great water'. Even though I knew that Gods world and my world were the same in love, my mind kept separating them, by putting Gods world outside of me. No wonder they say 'The Tao that can be explained, is not the eternal Tao.' I had forgotten that everything only exists in the present moment; I had put time into the equation and went looking as though on a journey. I had forgotten that everything just is in this moment; I had again created a separate me.

Meanwhile I was still in the rehab, and had rung the halfway house to tell my friend what had happened. Out of twelve people who live at the house only one attends Alcoholics Anonymous meetings regularly, and he was always asking me if I would like to go to meetings with him, He gave me the shits, I used to call him Mr AA, and not in a nice way. I wanted nothing to do with what I thought was a religious organization; It was Mr AA who answered the phone.

I reckon I know all about AA. When I was living in the parks in Townsville, I went to the Sally's for a loaf of bread and a tin of baked beans, they asked me to sort some clothes, I didn't mind that but when I went to collect my food they asked if I would like to go to a meeting, being hungry I agreed, but as I entered the room I was confronted by a large banner hanging from the wall, on the top of the banner was the word GOD in very large red letters, instantly I turned, "I'm not going to any fucking church, even for a bakery full of bread, you can stick your fucken bread, you know where." I was out of there as fast as I could go. Much later I found this to be an AA meeting, and the banner was the serenity prayer, which hangs on the wall in all AA meeting rooms. It had nothing to do with the Salvos at all; AA had just rented the room.

Anyway Mr AA, his name was Geoff by the way, did what he always did, he offered to come out to the rehab and take me to a meeting, I had given up fighting, and anyway I would be able to tell them that they have got the wrong idea about God. I agreed, why not go?

The meeting was held in a large hall, fifty or sixty people were there, and members were being called to walk out to the front of the hall and stand next to a table where the chairman of the meeting sat facing the congregation of alcoholics seated in rows all the way to the back of the hall. When called to the front, each member identified him or herself as being 'Joe or Ann, and I'm an alcoholic.' Each member was sharing their experience, strength, and hope, telling what it was like, what happened, and what it is like now. I didn't understand a lot of what was said, at least I didn't think I did, my brain was still pretty well fried, and AA has terms that I hadn't heard before. Don't forget, after all what's happened, I still wasn't giving up on the idea of learning to drink in moderation. Members were saying things like, 'it's the first drink that does the damage,' and 'One's too many and a hundred is not enough.' I was sitting about halfway towards the back, and remember thinking that they have that wrong, it's about the twentieth drink that does the damage.

Toward the end of the meeting the chairman called me to share; I was feeling fairly confident, after all, hadn't I just had a spiritual experience, and wasn't I going to put them right about God?

I walked to the front, stood behind the chair that was there to sit on if one wanted, but I had noticed that no one sat on it, I was standing there holding the back of the chair, and when I looked out at all of the people, every bit of my confidence evaporated, my legs turned to jelly, I started to shake all over, I held the back of the chair for support, and the chair vibrated across the tiled floor like a Jack Hammer, I was terrified, I wanted to say "My name's Ron and I'm an alcoholic," just like everyone else had done. As I got to the word alcoholic, it stuck in my throat, It wouldn't come out, and while I stood there shaking, my thoughts went back to all of the times that I had stopped drinking, the times when I had locked myself away from alcohol in the bush, or at sea, or the time I spent a whole year away from alcohol using Vallium and dope. I saw before me that first drink, the one that does the damage, every time I had that first drink I lost control and it wasn't too long before I was in a mess. All of this took only a moment, it was like my life passing before my eyes, and as I stood there, I realised "I can't drink, I just can't drink, I can't drink ever." As I saw this, the word alcoholic that had been stuck, came free, and with it so did I. Then the voice again "it will be alright'. The denial left me at that moment, and I felt like I had landed in the middle of a room of alcoholics just like me, I wasn't separate any longer, and the craving for alcohol left.

Inspirations

Hope

In the book 'Alcoholics Anonymous' it states. 'We have recovered from a hopeless state of mind and body'. We don't have to be an alcoholic to be suffering from this devastating state of being. There many who suffer without hope, but there is a solution. The twelve steps of Alcoholics Anonymous are now being used by over one hundred different organizations throughout the world. If you are suffering from, a mental disorder, eating disorder, or any of the hundred other disorders, you may find hope in one of the twelve step programs. Information is available via the internet. May you find peace.

Living in love with you eternally

Ronald Russell   Namaste'

Chapter Twenty Four

At that first meeting of Alcoholics Anonymous, a chap had shared about getting a sponsor, He was very well dressed, and was quoting from the Big Book of Alcoholics Anonymous, commonly called the Big Book, I thought he must be one of the heads of AA. After the meeting, being very interested in AA all of a sudden, I asked him what a sponsor was, my brain was fried but I had played and followed sports, and I knew that a sponsor paid for all the equipment and things. "Do I have to get someone to pay my way into AA" I asked. He smiled "No, a sponsor is someone who will guide you through the twelve steps of AA and the traditions, he will generally help with any problems you come across." I was very interested, "How do I get a sponsor?" I asked. "It's not too hard, just go to a few different meetings, and you will come across someone that you think might be able to help you, and if he hasn't got too much on he will take you on." Well, here I was with one of the leaders of AA, so out of the blue I asked "Will you be my sponsor?" "I'd love to;" he picked up a brand new Big Book from the table and handed it to me, "This is not just a book, this is your life, I want you to read this book from the preface right through, but first I would like you to read the chapters, 'How it works' and 'A vision for you.' And if you get this program pass this book on to another newcomer as I did for you. I have passed on many books since that day. Oh, and by the way, there are no leaders in AA, 'Our leaders are but trusted servants'.

Brian my sponsor, took me to my first meeting outside of the rehab, it was in a church, at this meeting I shared that I 'KNEW' that I would never drink again. After the meeting a few older sober members came to me saying that I can't say that, "this program is one day at a time" they told me. Well I didn't care about that, I did know, deep in my heart I knew, that I would never drink again, they kept on, and I started thinking 'Fuck these old bastards, I know what I know, if they think that they will drink again, well that's their friggen problem,' I might have had a spiritual experience, but I had a lot of buttons left to push. I was thinking 'Who gives a shit, I don't need this any way, I can do this by myself.' I was walking toward the door, when a woman about the same age as me appeared right in front of me, I hadn't seen her and almost walked into her, she had her arms outstretched, and smiling, she welcomed me into a hug. This was the most loving hug I had experienced since I had left my mother, and as she hugged me she whispered "You can say whatever you feel is right." In an instant I felt at peace, I felt at home. I still say today, "I was loved into AA, and love has kept me here.

My sponsor took me through the twelve steps of AA and as I did them I realised how much shit I had in my life. The fourth step showed me how to uncover all my defects of character, and in the fifth I had to share this with God and another human being, 'I chose my sponsor.' So basically, without going through all of the 12 steps here, I had to accept what is stated in the Big Book of AA in chapter five.

> That we were alcoholic, and our lives had become unmanageable.
> That probably no human power could relieve our alcohol.
> That God could and would if He were sought.

The twelfth step states that having had a spiritual awakening as the result of these steps, we tried to carry this message to alcoholics, and to practise these principles in all our affairs.

My biggest problem was that I had had a spiritual experience, and that was enough for my ego to grab hold of and run with. It would reason, that having had the experience I didn't need an awakening.

The experience was exactly that, an experience, I had experienced God. The rest of the program was to teach me to allow the God of my understanding to guide my life. Rather than a program of learning, it became a program of un-learning all of the knowledge that I was taught, and replace it with spiritual wisdom, in AA, for me it is not a new improved old life, it is a brand new life built on spiritual principles, and my new life is still evolving for me today. We have a saying, 'My best thinking got me to the doors of AA, and God can handle the rest.' There are so many benefits from this program, I have never been happier than I am today and I get a chance to see others recovering from this disease. Today while writing this, it is the second of September 2015 and I'm just over thirty one years sober, only this morning a chap came up to me, shaking and nervous asking me to be his sponsor through the program of AA, and two days ago on Saturday Lisa, a thirty eight year old sponsee, invited me to a lunch of fish and chips on the beach at Hervey Bay, after a couple of wonderful hours, she handed me a card as we parted with our usual hug, these are the words written on the card.

Dear Ronnie,

Thank you so much for being my rock, friend and all that you are. Mostly for believing in me. You are an amazing soul and I'm constantly in awe of all that you do and are. More importantly. "I love you" Big hug, Lisa xox.

There have been many such sentiments over the years, from both men and women, from people just like me who knew nothing of spiritual love, who knew only darkness, before AA, and each one leaves my heart singing. I'm sharing this, not through ego, but to humbly give thanks for something I have been freely given, I have been given what I have today despite myself. I have no religion, my religion is Love. But Jesus said something like 'Don't hide your light under a bowl, let it shine so that others can see it and let their light shine also.' And that's easy to do today, because it is not my light that's shining.

To get to this place, my story has quite a few years to run, and because of my inability to trust in Love, they have at times been very difficult years.

'Wisdom is experience learned.'

It was time to leave the half way house, and I'd saved and bought a caravan, which I had transported to a caravan park overlooking the ocean at Main Beach on the beautiful Gold Coast. I had no car or licence; I let my licence go almost five years before. There's quite a few bottles bought for the price of a licence. A second hand shop had a small girl's bike which I purchased, and put the seat up as far as it would go, it was, I suppose quite funny seeing a six foot one skinny rake riding a ten year olds, girlie bike around the Gold Coast, my AA friends wouldn't be seen dead with me while I was riding my bike. My friends and I would attend up to three meetings each day, walking to many of them and being driven to others.

My Taoist studies with the I Ching, The Tao Te Ching and Tai Chi, led me to a course in Traditional Chinese Medicine. A four year degree course, I had a lot of trouble at first but my memory seemed to be able to cope long enough to pass the exams. At the end of the second year I heard of master practitioner who had set up a teaching, and hands on clinic at Burleigh Heads. This to me was a dream come true, I learnt so much more than I would have learnt at college. I learnt about the spiritual points of acupuncture, something I had not heard of. While at the college I learnt Iridology, Chinese massage, Shiatsu, and not long ago, I became a Reiki Healing Master. Before I was six years sober I had completed a two year Queensland state department of health drug and alcohol counselling course.

A lot of members had nick names on the Gold Coast, A real estate agent was called Real Estate John, Another who quoted from the Big Book was called Big Book Russell, I was called spiritual Ron, because I was always sharing about the spiritual side of the program. A small band of us travelled around the Coast sharing at different meetings, and it was at one of these meetings that Heather, my future wife heard me share, she told me a few months later after we had become an item that I was the first person who had a similar understanding of a higher power as she did, and that she was going to marry me, she, like me, didn't agree with any religions. I didn't know any of this at the time, and I didn't know that another member friend of mine was her brother. We were sitting on side seats in the community hall when Heather was called to share; Wow! She had mid length wavy red hair and was dressed in a white blouse with a very short tartan skirt and red stiletto heel shoes. Glen, her brother was always ribbing me about women and as Heather walked to the front he tried again, "How'd you like to go with that," he was nudging me in the side. I was embarrassed, I was terrified of women, I was looking at the floor "Come over after the meeting and I'll introduce you to her, I know her well." As I said earlier, he didn't let on that he was her brother, I didn't know what to say, I didn't feel that anyone as beautiful as this woman would be interested in me; the old days at the dance halls were with me again, and I didn't want to be made a fool.

Ron, "I'd like you to meet Heather," It was Glens voice, I turned to be met by the most captivating smile, I don't use the word captivating lightly, I was captured. It wasn't until Heather and I started dating did I get the whole story about how she heard me share and got her brother to introduce us. I had recently done a ten day silent retreat in Vipassana meditation, and had given up smoking, there was no doubt that Heather was a most beautiful woman, so one day I got really romantic and said "If you give up smoking and do a retreat with me, we could get married." It's a wonder I didn't get a brick around my head. All I got was that wonderful Heathery smile as she looked up from her five foot three inches. "Let's do it," We were married that year on Boxing Day 1988, with well over a hundred guests and no alcohol, two sober alcoholics beginning a life together on life's terms.

Inspirations

Peace comes to the world, not by good overcoming evil, but by realising and accepting, good and evil, life and death, are necessary for the harmony of the universe.

Living in love with you eternally

Ronald Russell   Namaste'

Chapter Twenty Five

For the two years leading up to my marriage, I was on a pink spiritual cloud; I was sharing things at meetings that many had not heard before, Eckhart Tolle type stuff, most people in those days were into fundamental type spirituality, I was sharing I am God / Love and that was fine while I was single, living by myself I had no one to press my buttons and I could hide safely under my veil of spirituality. Members at meetings would share saying there's one thing you need to know, and that is, that there is a God and its not you, I would smile to myself, thinking how little they knew. Oh, yes, I would try to share that God is Love, or Love is God, and because we are created in God's image we must be that Love. That didn't go down too well in those early days, but it is much more accepted these days.

My biggest problem was that I had to be right, we have a saying in AA 'Live and let live' I didn't understand that at all, another one was. 'Would you rather be right or be happy?' My answer to that would be 'Right' because when I'm right I'm happy. I had an ego bigger than Ben Hur, and every time I did a good deed, my ego would grab hold of it and run, I'm very lucky there are traditions in AA aimed at keeping us humble; otherwise my ego would have me standing for AA member of the year.

Heather came into my life at just the right time, she pulled me back to earth, and we became a very good team, although it took some time. I wasn't aware then that I had so many buttons to push, and Heather pushed every one more than once. I hadn't realised just how selfish I was, having lived by myself for so long, I had no idea how to share me. Even though we worked well together, there were a lot of fights, but we had the program of AA and gradually we came to live life on life's terms, or as Goenka, the Vipassana meditation teacher would say "As it is, not as you would like it to be."

Possibly, the most important people in our lives are the ones who push our buttons, I'm really grateful to all who have pushed my buttons, thereby allowing me to become aware of my faults. You know, I was always led to believe that our faults were bad and had to be gotten rid of, but today I know that is not possible, Faults are a part of our human existence, the good, the bad, and the ugly. As I become aware of them and see them for what they are, they lose their value and don't affect me any longer. Everything in the human existence is made of opposites, we can't have mountains without valleys, heaven without earth, how would we know joy if we didn't have sadness to compare it to.

To realise that all these opposites are illusions, is maybe what some call enlightenment, but I know from my experience that if the enlightened person thinks he is the enlightened person, at that moment, he is not the enlightened person. Sounds crazy, but to me it is the truth as I know it. But again I digress, back to the story.

Many times in my sobriety, pictures of my children John and Rita, would enter my head, I would see a child on a bus and wonder if that could be one of them, once outside a picture show I saw two children about the same age as John and Rita the last time I saw them, only to realise that they would be grown into teenagers now. I was still living in my van not long before Heather and I got married, when John contacted me, he was now eighteen years old, he had got hold of me through the social security, and wanted to know if he could bring Rita down to see me. I was over the moon and at the same time very nervous, but my rock, Heather stood by me and her enthusiasm about meeting my children stilled my fears.

Over nine years had passed, and as I stood at the bus stop I was wondering if I would recognise them, John was easy to recognise, a very handsome darker version of me with his slightly bent nose, and loping walk, just like mine. I suppose I recognised Rita more because she was with John at first, and even though I hadn't seen her since she was six, there was no mistaking her beautiful smile and wide sparkling eyes, I can tell you my heart was singing, and it was a very proud dad that hugged his children that day. The fear came back again as soon as we got back home, were they angry about my leaving without a word nine years before? They said not, but all I could do was make amends, and the best way to do that was to be a sober dad. The sober bit was easy, but I had no idea about how to be a dad, I had never really been one, Rita was only fifteen, I think, and had found friends who were taking her out drinking, John was much more stable and was worried about her. My trouble was, seeing as I had never been a father, what right did I have now to pull them into line, all I felt I could do was support John in being the older brother. Heather had won them over and we had a short but very enjoyable reunion. Later I travelled to Townsville and made amends to Emily as best I could, but she had another life. Much later my other son Ronald found me thirty one years after he was born, I travelled back to TI to meet him for the first time since he was only six months old, one thing that has always amazed me is how handsome, and beautiful these children turned out. I have no doubts that my children were hurt by my alcoholism, and possibly their children as well, but that is their story.

Inspirations

Please don't judge me for having a God of my own understanding. If we are truly honest with ourselves, we will find each of us have our own concept of what god is or isn't. This separate concept will continue until we awake from the dream of the 'human' condition and become the oneness of 'BEing'.

Living in love with you eternally

Ronald Russell   Namaste'

Chapter Twenty Six

When I met Heather I was working out of my caravan as a natural therapist. My card read, 'Altered Attitudes Natural Therapies Centre', followed by all the diplomas and certificates I had, I had built the annex specifically for this purpose, it was light and airy but private with a massage table neatly tucked at the back end, with relaxing music playing it was a pleasant place to be while being treated. Heather was driving a pie van for her sister around the Kirra and Robina areas of the Gold Coast, and I would give her a hand sometimes. It was on one of these occasions that we noticed a sign on a corner shop, right opposite the Kirra hotel and directly across from the beach. Caretaker needed for three units and two shops. We made an arrangement that we would look after the complex and in return we could have the vacant shop rent free. Heather came from a business orientated family, and was a qualified florist. We sold the caravan and set up a florist business with one corner used for natural therapies. We called it 'Flowers and Therapies,' I helped Heather with the flowers and Heather became my nurse.

Heather would drive the pie van sometimes when her sister was sick. I realised how much money was to be made, and that the coast was growing very fast. For two thousand dollars, I built my own pie van, got it registered for food safety and went out to new building sites to find clients. Within a month we were making twice the money that the florist and clinic made together. At this stage Heather and I started fighting a lot, we were working too hard and under a lot of stress, Heather was diagnosed as being menopausal and with treatment her moods improved dramatically. Heather was also an insulin dependent diabetic, and when her blood sugars got low her moods became impossible, I didn't understand this at first and would react angrily, and it got so bad that we started sleeping apart.

All of this on top of a spiritual experience, where had all the love gone? It didn't make sense. What happened to the steps where we asked God to remove our shortcomings? I seemed to have more now than ever. It took a few more years to realise that I didn't want them removed, maybe a bit but not all of them, I needed to have control, even the anger was a way of controlling others, I suppose it was like giving up the alcohol I was afraid to let go, and trust that 'it will be all right'. There are those words again.

Counselling didn't work, Heather said the counsellor was biased towards me, and I would reply that proves that I'm right. Really I find it difficult that people can't see that I'm always right. I'm convinced that if more did, the world would be a better place. I suppose everyone has the right to be wrong.

We were close to breaking up, and decided to sit down and talk it out as calmly as possible, we put a microphone and tape recorder on the table, and made a commitment we would hold nothing back, and that we would not interrupt the other while they were speaking. We spoke about what we wanted from our relationship, what each of us thought had to be done, and how to do it. We spoke about whether we should separate for a short while or for good. Tears were flowing freely as we voiced our wants and needs, and after quite some time, we were exhausted, and everything, every sob, every angry word, every cry for recognition was on the tape. We were too exhausted to play it back so decided to wait until tomorrow, but it had already done some good, it allowed us to see, if only in a small way, where we were coming from. We slept together that night for the first time in a while, and we realised, no matter what was going on we still loved each other, although sometimes the love looked like hate.

The next day there were more tears, as we realised the pain each of us were in, but in the end one thing came out of it that stood out above all else. What we both wanted was the Australian dream, a little cottage in the country with a few animals, a beautiful garden and a white picket fence and peace.

All our plants were in pots and my dream was to plant them in the ground, once and for all. We decided to do a ten day Vipassana retreat to clear our minds then sell the pie van and get a camper, In the meantime while we were in meditation Paul, Heathers son and his girlfriend would look after the pie run.

All worked out well and we sold our two thousand dollar van for twenty seven thousand dollars. We threw a double bed mattress into the back of an old van and took off to find our dream home. 'Everything was all right'

There were a lot of lovely homes which fitted the bill perfectly, but all were all just outside our price range, and with everything added together and with what we could borrow, we could only raise fifty nine thousand dollars. One afternoon, I was bought home to the reality of where we were. While sitting on the mattress in the back of the van, surrounded by plans, maps and real estate pamphlets. I thought out loud "I can't wait to get home and sort all this stuff out." I was pointing at the array of pamphlets on the mattress.

"We are home", Heather pointed out. "This is where we live." It was a shock; after all of the houses we had looked at, this is as far as we had come, home on a mattress in the middle of nowhere.

Maryborough, the one place we had missed on the way up north, Glen, Heathers brother had played golf here once and said that it was very hot. It was about one hundred miles south from us, so we decided to check it out. Maryborough is called the heritage city, jam packed with old Queenslanders and stately old homes, we fell in love instantly. If only we can find something here, so many beautiful homes but the ones that suited were just out of reach. Then driving along the river we came across a beautiful high set four bedroom Queenslander with a 'For private sale' on the fence. The owner was working in the yard so we asked the price. "I've just now put the sign up, its part of my family's deceased estate. There's another quarter acre block under separate title adjoining this, I want fifty two for this and eighteen for the block. I'd like to sell them both together if possible." We offered what we had, that was fifty nine for the two, but he refused. "Tell you what I'll do, I'll sell you the house for fifty two, and if you can find another ten, you get them both for sixty two," Wow, what a deal, someone up there likes us. The house alone was underpriced by fifteen thousand dollars. We shook on it, promising to come back immediately with a thousand dollars deposit if he takes the sign down.

It took a while to find the three thousand dollars we were short. Heathers mum was thinking about loaning us the money, but was taking for ever to make up her mind. In the meantime Cathy, Heathers daughter was having her third daughter in Brisbane; we went down to look after the first two while she had Samantha. I was in the Valley and decided to buy a system seven lotto ticket, I just wrote the numbers as the came to my head. That night we won three thousand three hundred dollars. The exact amount we needed, the more you notice how things fall into place and show gratitude the more these things happen. A year later we sold the block for twenty five thousand and bought a disused Sunday school on a paddock, sitting all by itself, for seventeen thousand, this I turned into a beautiful dwelling using recycled timber.

There was a lot of recycled timber around Maryborough, and a lot of people were getting rid of their old wooden furniture and replacing it with stainless steel and glass. Heather and I were in our element, we both loved old wooden furniture and made a little sideline business out of it, I had let natural therapies go, but it was working in our lives, we lived a very healthy lifestyle, meditating daily and attending a ten day silent retreat each year, most of our children would attend now and again, I have done about ten retreats and I think Paul has done more. Every year or two we would buy a house, renovate it and sell it for a profit, I have just purchased my tenth house.

Inspirations

What would the master do?

It's so easy to love the loveable, but how do we love those not so easy to love? There are many problems in life, which the right answers don't seem to be forth coming. Today I ask myself the simple question. "What would the Master do?' It matters not who or what the master is to you. The answer is always there, and we will intuitively know it is the right answer.

Living in love with you eternally

Ronald Russell   Namaste'

Chapter Twenty Seven

Tea trees were the big fad and money maker; a couple of friends were growing them and suggested we have a go. To us, being interested in natural therapies, it seemed the perfect way to go. We put our home on the market and with the same agent put in an order for a property of around fifty acres. The home sold one week before the property became available. We were now the proud owners of fifty acres of land, with a three bedroom house a very large shed, tractor, spring fed dams, kangaroos, and heaps of snakes. More than one of the grand children would find a snake in their wardrobe or coiled up in a corner of their room. Cathy had a fright one night when she went to put the kettle on for coffee in the middle of the night, she had decided to leave the light off so as not to disturb anyone, and while feeling for the kettle felt something strange, and pulling back quickly she turned on the light, only to find an eastern brown snake curled around the base and handle of the kettle.

All we had to do now was to turn the property into a tea tree plantation with very little money, but that was our speciality, we were experts at doing the almost impossible with almost nothing.

Paul, Heather's eldest son, I call all Heathers children mine, or our, I leave out the step, and they call me Ron. I thought that Ron or Ronnie as they often call me, would be less intrusive on the children and grand children than dad or step dad, especially when there were a couple of real dads still on the scene. Anyway, Paul was an invaluable help in all of our enterprises, he had a very sharp mind and often came up with answers to problems that had us baffled, he would stay for a while, and help restore a house or some furniture, then move on to something of his own for a while, and be back when we needed him.

We only paid about half the value of the property because of the poor condition the house was in. No one had lived in the place for two years and teenagers used to drive out to the property and party on. Unfortunately the power was off so the pump that supplied water to the toilet didn't work, that left us with a toilet full to over flowing with excrement and vomit. Heather couldn't even walk into the house it was so bad. I could handle things like that, I just made my mind up to do it and then I would bite the bullet and do it, although I found myself dry reaching a few times.

I was reminded of a time when I was working in Townsville at the prawn factory as the maintenance engineer. In those days there were still some outside dunnies (Toilets with a drum to catch the waste) and the excrement from these would be emptied into large holes about ten feet in diameter and four and a half feet deep. The shells and heads from the prawns would have to be transported out to these holes and buried. Our truck had slipped off the narrow road between the holes and become bogged, and it was my job to go out there and get it free. The truck had to be jacked up, and as I walked around the side with the jack I walked on what looked like solid ground, but was actually a hole full of shit which had dried to a crust on top and had been covered with dust, making it look like solid ground. I was up to my chest in the stuff, what was I to do? I still had to get the truck out and it was much easier to place the jack from that position, I stayed there until we got the truck free, and because both I and the truck were covered in shit I drove it back to the factory. Unfortunately the only way back was through the main street in town and by the time we arrived, there were already complaints arriving from the town folk about the condition and smell of the truck.

Paul, Heather and I got the house liveable, and the machinery working. The chemistry books from my natural therapies course came in handy with a drawing of a glass still. I just enlarged this to design and build my own still. It was made from a disused five hundred gallon steel diesel tank, and stainless pipe I collected from a scrap yard. We had plenty of firewood to heat the water into the steam which passed through the mulched tea trees, taking with it the precious oil, which was then condensed and separated into water and the oil which floated on the water. The commercial still cost around thirty thousand dollars, mine cost five hundred, and cost nothing to run, what's more, we were getting a better recovery from our trees, than the commercial stills were. I'll always remember the first drops of oil that came from that still, Heather, Paul and I were dancing hand in hand around the still, whooping and hollering like Indians doing a war dance. That was the culmination of two years of very hard work, it was absolutely exciting.

To get to that point, and to carry on farming, took a lot of effort from many people in our extended family, John, my son would come down from Townsville and help with harvesting and marketing, Even Rita and her kids came to help, later on Cathy and her partner Jason came to stay with their new born son, and help as well.

There was a lot of dysfunction in the family due to the alcoholism, and for a long time, Heather and I found ourselves bringing up our, at that time five grandchildren on the farm. They actually grew up on that property, which I believe helped them grow into well balanced beautiful adults, that and the never ending unconditional love Heather bestowed upon them. I remember one argument Heather and I had over the children, we were going through years of court cases over residency of the children and I felt that it was preventing us from making our first million dollars. I asked Heather why we couldn't give the children back after a visit like other grandparents do. Heather just looked at me and asked "How do I do that?" she had me there and then, at that stage the choice for the children was us, drugging parents, or foster care. From that moment on I decided to support Heather all the way in her dealing with the family. She was the Matriarch, and the benefits I received from that decision are still with me today, especially in the areas of being able to love, without fear.

Being able to love without fear may sound a little strange, I mean there is no fear in love is there, but it was only a few years ago, that Heather was crouching in our lounge room, head between her hands sobbing until her slender body was shaking. "What's wrong with me, you never say you love me anymore?" Heather looked up with those sad, tear filled eyes "do you love me?" Looking down at Heather, my heart was breaking, I just wanted to pick her up in my arms and hold her as close as I possibly could, I wanted to tell her that I loved her more than she could ever imagine, But even though my heart was breaking the fear of what would happen if I said I loved her was too great, fear was telling me that I would become vulnerable, and that the love could be used against me. That same fear answered, "Well I married you didn't I?" It took many years to learn how to trust completely. Today I have that love within so strong that at times my heart feels like it will burst, and who knows, if I had no one to share it with, it might do just that. I'm just so grateful to have my life just as it is today.

Seventy thousand tea trees were planted by hand in ten acres of the property; the kids would come home from school, change clothes and come down to the paddock and help plant. Day after day, week after week, month after month, we planted and after two years we had our tea tree plantation all ready to harvest. There was one problem, when we decided to go into tea trees the price of oil was sixty dollars per litre, but because of interest by the large corporations the market was flooded and the price dropped to ten dollars per litre.

My knowledge of chemistry and natural therapies was put to good use again, and by designing new mixtures and products we were able to get one hundred dollars per litre. To get this we had to attend weekly markets to sell our products. The children would help with the selling gaining valuable experience in that area as well.

Meanwhile Paul had decided to live permanently on the property, so I drew up council plans and Paul and I built an amazing log cabin using our own trees, Paul also furnished it with timber from the property. After a few years he left and the cabin became a sanctuary for family members needing somewhere to have a break from the stresses of life.

There was a lot going on in our lives and both Heather and I gradually stopped going to our AA meetings, we would still read AA and spiritual literature and every now and again I would take a friend or a family member to a meeting, but before long AA was forgotten. About this time Phil, Heathers step son whom I had taken to many rehabs and had been trying to get sober for years, fell out of the door of a hotel on one of his busts and cracked his head. He was taken to hospital unconscious, but because he had been taken there many times blind drunk, the staff just thought that this was the same, and never checked him out properly, "Its only Phil again he'll be right in the morning." Phil's brain had ruptured and by the time they had flown him to Brisbane the next day it was too late to do anything, he never regained consciousness and we visited him in an old people's home daily until his death six months later. Phil was only forty years old.

Without meetings and with all that was going on fear began to creep back into my life. We were being threatened by the children's father, telling us that his bikie, drug dealing mates were coming to get us. The fears of the days up on Horn Island were returning, and I couldn't see it. All around the property, hidden behind trees were sharpened steel pickets and sharpened steel rods to use as spears, and closer by I had filled spray bottles full of battery acid in case of attack, although I never told anyone about these, the frightening thing is, I know that I would have used them. All of this after having had a spiritual experience, and over one hundred hours of meditation retreat.

I was getting older, close to sixty and it was becoming too hard to work the property by hand, even the trees were cut separately by hand because we couldn't afford a harvester, so we decided to sell. Because it was a going concern we got a good price, and because Heather wanted to help Cathy buy a house we split the money so that she could use her half for that purpose.

Inspirations

Dawn is just starting to paint the sky with its pearly hue, I'm up early this morning, quietly sitting and allowing the harmony of all that is flow throughout. I feel the cool fresh breeze on my bare arms, and I smell the freshness that this breeze brings from the fields along the nearby river. The early birds are starting their song, and in the distance a rain bird calls its mate, It will rain in three days, it is probably right, I notice the ants hurriedly moving to higher ground, Sunny Boy the Golden Labrador lazily wanders over, licks at my hand to let me know he is here, I look down into the depths of the most loving golden brown eyes, for a moment we connect, we are one, the moment passes but is not lost, he is happy to settle at my feet, no sound, no words, just a silent knowing all is as it should be, my heart is singing and I know we are living in love and harmony with all that is.

Living in love with you eternally

Ronald Russell   Namaste'

Chapter Twenty Eight

While Heather was house hunting with Cathy, I found another old house in the small township of Bauple, about thirty minutes south of Maryborough; it was the right price but what a mess. Drunks and drug addicts had been living in this house, along with the white ants. At one stage in its life it had been lined with beautiful cedar timber, but there was a story that the old bloke who built it had hidden his money in the house before he died. The drunks and addicts had pulled the cedar from the walls in search of the money and unfortunately had burnt it in their cooking fires. The house was in such bad condition that when I asked a builder friend of mine what he would do with it he said that he would bulldoze it and start again.

With help, a lot of it from my son John, I turned it into one of the most beautiful homes in the district, and Heather's gardens set everything off to perfection. Heather came up with the idea of a food van for the local markets, so after gaining permission from the powers to be I set out to build our food van from a classic 1960 ten foot caravan. It was only small but I managed to fit a food warmer, Deep fryer, Fairy floss machine, Hot dog maker, Milk shakes, fridge and soft drinks. Then seeing we were going to the markets we decided to get a jumping castle and call the business 'Kids Partys' We ended up with five castles and a very lucrative business.

Heathers health had started to go downhill, just little things at first, an attack of Tackardia now and then, peripheral damage to her feet due to her long term diabetes, and more and more she found herself falling backwards for no apparent reason.

Heather stopped coming to the markets, and it wasn't much fun without her, so we sold the business and retired. It was so peaceful sitting in our cane chairs on the veranda watching the world go by, getting visits from the grand children, and being able to give them back to their parents after the visit. I had started back at AA and the world was rosy.

I was unloading the weeks supply of groceries from the back of the van, when I heard a short cry and glanced across to see Heather falling backwards from the top of the five steps leading up to our front veranda, the fall seemed to be happening in slow motion, and I got to her just as she hit the bottom, she didn't even put out her hands to break the fall. I was thinking that her head had hit one of the garden rocks just beside her head, and she was screaming the scream that can only mean intense pain, Heather had landed on her back and the first point of contact with the ground was her spine just between her shoulder blades. There was no blood so I was hoping she hadn't hit her head, then the screaming stopped as she passed out, I was so, so, afraid. I had no idea where she was hurt, so I picked her up and carried her to the cane lounge where she usually sat and relaxed. I was looking for the key to let us inside so that I could get her to bed when she woke up. I was instantly beside her asking where she was hurting, I had a million questions, and while I was looking into her eyes they rolled to the back showing only the whites, then closed. Heather stopped breathing, and the fear welled up inside me, "Oh no, Heather, Heather," I was shaking her "I've lost her, oh no, Heather." Indescribable fear, then with a deep breath she was awake, but the fear wouldn't leave me.

"I'm, alright she was telling me, just hurt my back; a couple of paracetamol will help."

"Ok, but I'm calling the ambulance, you really scared me, I thought you died a minute ago."

"No, don't call the ambulance, I'm not going to the hospital, I'll be ok, just get me to the bed, after you roll me a smoke" Heathers fear was not of the hospital but on not being able to smoke while in hospital, her smoking was the cause of all our arguments, and it was no different this time, and I told her how selfish she was, worrying me by not going to hospital. One moment I'm terrified I'm losing the love of my life the next I'm accusing her of making my life miserable, strange world?

Heather was in so much pain the next morning that she agreed to go to the hospital, but only to get a prescription for stronger pain killers, once there, they x-rayed her back, then admitted her into a ward, I went out and bought some nicotine patches, to make her stay a little easier.

The x-rays showed that she had cracked a bone in her spine, but they wanted to do more scans to find out why she was falling so often.

Shock of all shocks they had found a Pancoast Tumour on the top of her lungs, and possibly another in the area where the back had been broken, the doctor was very kind with a wonderful compassionate manner. I suggested that I would build a Granny flat underneath Cathy's hi-set house, but when I told the doctor that it would take three months he shook his head, and in a soft kind way told me that I might not have that long, as this type of tumour is very aggressive. Heather didn't want to tell the grand children, but again the doctor explained to her that seeing as they were grown up, it wouldn't be fair to keep this from them. Heather kept asking me if this meant that she was going to die, and all I could say is what the doctor said, and that was that it depends on whether they could operate successfully, and that a biopsy would be the first step.

We hear of everyone around us getting cancer and because it's not us, or really close to us, we pay little attention, now that it had hit us we were finding out just how many of our friends have gone through, or are going through this cancer experience. The natural remedies started pouring in from friends and family, but Heather was on so much medication already, and now with the added medication from this hospitalization she felt she couldn't take any more, and we had to ask people to stop sending it.

The Biopsy was taken in the Royal Brisbane Women's Hospital, and because of Heathers smoking she got a chest infection, and pneumonia, she was very close to death and it was so painful watching her trying to breath that I was wishing it would end, sometimes I could hear her laboured breathing even before entering the ward.

Heather was in this bad state when her brother, Glen came to visit, he broke down completely saying over and over "Why her, why Heather, she has only shown love towards everyone, it should be me."

Being honest, I don't think anyone thought that she would last the week, but thankfully it's not up to us what God or the universe has in store. Coincidentally, at this very moment Glen must have been riddled with undiagnosed cancer and he passed away around six months later.

Heather was placed in the palliative care ward, and we were gently told that she would not survive this but there need be no pain, the pain management in palliative care was second to none, and so were the doctors and especially the nurses, as Heather wasn't always the best patient, she had bouts of anger especially about her diabetic management, and usually she was right. Long term diabetics seem to be able to manage their diabetes much better than hospital staff that have to follow strict guidelines that don't always suit the patient, but over all they do an excellent job. Heather trusted me, even above the doctors and wouldn't allow any changes unless they were checked by me.

There was a long way to travel each day to the hospital, so we arranged to have Heather moved to another hospital closer to her daughters. This was more like a nursing home, not very large, and the rules were not so strict. Heather was encouraged to leave the sick bed and as much as possible live a normal life. It wasn't too long before we were taking her to outings in the park, and not long after that she was released, to come home. About eight months after she was diagnosed she was well enough to travel to Tasmania and spend three wonderful weeks with Paul and Hannah, we were back home for Christmas, where she was spoiled rotten.

We had begun to think that the cancer had gone as it wasn't showing up on the x-rays, But about six months after Tasmania things started to go wrong, she was hospitalised a couple more times and her blood platelets went haywire, she was becoming really difficult to look after at home, I was becoming more and more frustrated with her, she wouldn't do any exercise, I had trouble giving her the medication, sometimes I would prepare a really nice meal only to have her tip it out if I forced her to eat it. Honestly I was at my wits end; we were arguing over nothing, I wasn't coping at all.

Heather would throw the tablets at me if she didn't want to take them, and more than once I threw them back angrily. It all came to a head when she pushed a really nice meal away spilling some on the bed which I had to wash, I lost it completely I emptied the plate over her head and stormed out of the flat, I was fuming. Outside is a little patio where I sit for my quiet times and meditation, which by the way had slipped by the wayside. There was a pen and paper on the small table which I used to jot things down if they are bothering me; it's my way of getting things out of my head. I picked up the pen and began to write 'Why am I so angry at Heather, I know I love her, but I'm beginning to wish she was back in hospital so I don't have to look after her?' I put the pen down and just looked at the words I had written. Off the page and into my head came LOVE, I could see it clearly, UNCONDITIONAL LOVE, I could see that I was looking after Heather with selfish intent, I wanted Heather to get better, I wanted Heather to be easily managed, it had nothing to do with what Heather wanted, all I had to do was love Heather as she is, not to get her well, not to keep her alive, all this was not up to me, my job was to love, just love and make Heathers life as easy as possible. This was possibly the greatest epiphany I have had, I finally knew in my heart that I have no control, none whatsoever. This became for me the real meaning of the seventh step in AA. The second surrender.

After this awakening everything became easy, I was there to make Heathers passing journey as easy as possible, whatever she wanted I arranged for her to have, if possible. The elephant of death had left our relationship, and I could hold her hand and talk freely about where she wanted to be buried and that she would have to go into care when I could no longer care for her, these were such wonderful times, just living in love without any expectations. I'll have with me always the memory of the look of loving gratitude she gave me when I told her that, if she wanted, I would love to be buried beside her and Phil under the large tree in Tiaro cemetery, We had always talked about my ashes being scattered at sea, and when I mentioned the Tiaro cemetery she gave me that precious Heathery smile asking "Would you do that for me?"

It wasn't long before Heather was back in hospital for the last time. I would visit her as much as I possibly could and just sit beside her holding her hand and just be, she was often too tired to say anything, and there wasn't a lot to talk about any way, it had pretty well all been said, if we were lucky Heather would light up our day with one of her smiles, but they became less frequent each day, towards the end it felt like we had won the lotto when we got a Heathery smile. We knew the end was near and the night before she passed on I was able to tell her to let go, and that her job here was finished. My darling squeezed my hand and smiled, closed her eyes and slept.

The next morning I was called to the hospital, but arrived too late, she had already passed, and everyone was crying in the darkened room, I could see the look of worry in some of the eyes as to how I would handle this. They didn't know what Heather and I knew, and that was that we didn't die, it's only change. I touched her body and felt the already cool skin, and instantly knew that Heather wasn't in this cold, sad room. As I left the room into the sitting area I felt Heathers presence very strongly in the sunlight streaming in through the large glass windows that were the side wall of the waiting room. I find Heather everywhere I go, I only have to think of her and she is there in spirit, but we have one special meeting place, we discovered it many years ago in Queens Park in Maryborough, at the bottom of the park beside a walkway there's an old Morton bay fig tree, and hidden within its trunk and branches are small crevasses where the animals from 'Wind in the Willows' live, along with elves and fairies. I often meet with Heather there and watch our little friends play among the branches; I think they know we mean them no harm. I don't know, but maybe one has to believe in them to see them, like, we create our own reality don't we.

Inspirations

I have experienced the darkness and despair, and the fear this brings. I have experienced the light, and joy, and the love this brings. And this is alright for this is what human is. I am not my name, or photo on the wall, nor am I a cut out cardboard figure where my body finishes at the edge. No I am much than these. I am the air we breathe, the food we eat, the water we drink. I am the earth we walk on, the stars and the darkness and the light. But I am more than this, I am you, and you are me and we are love. And this is alright, for this is what human is.

Living in love with you eternally

Ronald Russell   Namaste'

Chapter Twenty Nine

I had always known that God was love, ever since my experience all those years ago, but I kept on separating the human from the spiritual; I was still living in the karma of yin and yang. Gradually I found myself being Love rather than giving Love, almost without awareness I found myself helping others, often simply by noticing their discomfort and finding myself comforting them. It has become so much easier to stand outside of myself and see the big picture, I find myself chuckling at the way I attach to people, places and things, even thoughts and opinions, I see life as a game that I shouldn't take too seriously, more importantly I see the oneness of all that is, and I see that there is no separation of the human and the spiritual, I see that there is no karma, and opposites do exist to this human mind, but not in the mind of God, where all is one, and all is Love, this is the place which no words can describe, it is a place where no journey can take you, and eternity is not enough time to get there. This is a place which is not a place, it is a nothingness which envelops everything, a place you will never go or ever leave, because it is you yourself, in life and in death, which in themselves are only words trying to word the unwordable.

To accept life as it is in this moment is very important to me. To live life in this human dream I must see and accept that there are ups and downs, there is good and bad, there are mountains and valleys, sadness and joy, the darkness and the light, and any opposite you would like to throw in. To see these as they really are and know that there is nothing wrong with either, to see good and evil as one, just as light and darkness are one, is to see life and death as one. If I accept good and evil as one, where can fear live?

This spiritual oneness is being kept alive through sharing this unconditional oneness, or as I like to call it today, Love, with others, I used to say other like minded people, but today I realise that we are all like minded. There are many, but there is one in particular who has helped me most. Rebecca asked me to sponsor her, about twenty five or six years old and so very beautiful, and there was a love that shone through the suffering, this made her so much more beautiful, and more than one fell in love with this shining light. Through support and validation Rebecca recovered enough to have a profound spiritual experience very similar to mine, but as I had no one to validate my experience, she had me.

Rebecca entered my life not long after I lost Heather, and her sharing of her experiences brought my experiences back to life, then as time went on I realised that Rebecca was experiencing things that I couldn't remember experiencing, it was as if she was opening doors that I had somehow closed, possibly through fear. Rebecca started sending me her daily journal, and I must admit, at times I became afraid for her, but when I mentioned this fear she asked me to trust her. I remember that I said to myself that I won't trust her but I'll trust God, same thing, I reasoned.

Because of the time that I have been practising this, I thought I could see the mistakes that Rebecca was making, especially when she would seem to lose all contact with the human form, that's when I became glad that I had put my trust in God rather than Rebecca. Today I know different, and that Rebecca was experiencing exactly what Rebecca had to experience, and whether she lived or died, it had nothing to do with anyone other than Rebecca and God. My job was to love Rebecca, unconditionally, I had forgotten so easily.

Probably the greatest thrill is that I'm still discovering my humanness, The Love has always been there, I'm discovering through my attachments the real human, and the excitement comes through this awakening, and the acceptance of it. There is no striving or fighting any longer, it is more like 'Allowing' myself to live in harmony with all that is, as it is.

In January 2015, after going to the dentist with a loose tooth, I was diagnosed as having oral cancer in the lower mouth, which extended from the front lip back to my tonsils and included part of my jaw and tongue. How could this be true, I drank apple cider vinegar every day to keep my acid level down, and had an amazing immune system, exercised daily and had a balanced diet, I haven't had a cold or flu for fifteen years.

It was explained that this was a result of my past life and was due to alcohol, tobacco and sun, I told the doctor that I hadn't been affected by these for over thirty years, and they explained that the twenty five years prior to my giving up alcohol and tobacco would have been more than enough to do the trick. Maybe he is right, or maybe there are things in life I'm still doing, in, what is called in the Buddhist tradition, 'Ignorance'. But even that is as it is, and I will or will not become aware in time.

My first reaction was that I don't need this; I might as well end it, I'm seventy three years old and I've had a full life. Then I realised that this wasn't my decision, I didn't know how to end it, or how to fix it, I remembered that life is a process and all I have to do is follow the process.

The operation was a major one, I think four and a half hours, but that is better than the nine hours that they were going to need for the throat dissection they had planned. They decided at the last minute to do the more simple operation, hoping to get everything in that. I'd like tell you another story about the higher power. I was few hours out from the operation, and recovering in intensive care, my mouth was full of packing and sewn shut to hold the graft in place, a feeding tube was fitted into one nostril and a breathing tube into the next. I love the saying….. "Whatever happens, I don't mind" but it's not the easiest thing to practise. The breathing tube became blocked with mucus and blood, so I couldn't breathe, I started to panic, I was completely helpless, I couldn't call for help, I was trying to use my eyes to attract attention, as my arms were strapped to my sides, the memory of drowning at Tamarama beach all those years ago entered my mind, then from seemingly out of nowhere the voice "Everything will be alright" I knew those words, although this time they had come from an intensive care nurse, they were the words I always heard when I thought I was in trouble, they were saying, 'trust me'. I'll always remember that nurse's name, Samantha W, because to me, that day, she was an angel, she cleared the tube and soothed my fear, wiping my brow, and comforting me with the words, "I'm here, and you are my only patient while you are in this ward, I won't leave you." And she was true to her word. To put it simply, Samantha had simply loved me unconditionally, and to me, that is the job of the Angels. My arms were freed and I was given a pad and pencil for communication, I found that Samantha, was on a spiritual journey, and I was able to recommend some helpful reading material. Samantha became a friend on Face book and a follower of my Face book page, Living in Love. We have now gone our own way, but she will never be forgotten.

Not long ago, I had the privilege of giving my daughter Vivienne away to Bernie a most pleasant and wonderful intensive care nurse, must be something about ICU nurses. This was the first time for me, I was able to dress up in a suit and tie, and be a part of regular society. I am so grateful to everyone who has entered my life, and for the gifts they have given me, I seem so far from that park bench, but in reality, it is only as far as the next drink.

December 2016

It's almost two years since my oral cancer operation; around six months ago another area of cancer showed up and was removed with surgery. One month after this surgery I asked the surgeon if it was likely to re-appear, "There's a good chance," he said. He was an excellent doctor and very honest. "We have removed everything at the moment, but there are no guarantees." I was a little taken back by this news, so I asked him "What's the use, why bother?" The doctor shook his head and replied with the perfect bedside voice "Everyone has a cross to bear." Well, I was feeling a little sorry for myself and thought this to be a bit harsh. Then, as I thought about all the people I know, I realised he was right. There were friends in wheelchairs, others with cancer, some with mental illness, and many with trauma that was invisible to the eye but affected them just as badly. Yes, everyone has a cross to bear.

This realisation helped a lot, and I was able to get off myself and get on with life. Only yesterday I was down for another check-up, and they found what they call Granulations on the floor of my mouth, but not enough to worry about at the moment, I'll go back in two months.

All this has helped me to live in the moment, I fully realise that this moment is all we have, and if I accept it as it is and not as I want it to be I'm finding an amazing peace.

My son and his two children have arrived from Townsville and we will celebrate Christmas together, then I'll spend some time with my second family.

I'm living in Hervey bay now, just across from the beach, and go swimming every morning after my meditation hour, I'm still attending AA meetings and I'm often reminded of the song "Amazing Grace" while gratefully living------

"A Life So Good"

That a drink won't make it better.

One last thing, over the years in recovery I noticed that there were a lot of people who, although not alcoholic could benefit from a twelve step program, so I decided to write a small booklet in the hope of reaching those in need. Following is the manuscript of the booklet which is separately available at Amazon books.

God Doesn't Live In The Fridge

INTRODUCTION

This book was inspired through my recovery from alcoholism and other devastating problems, such as gambling, overeating, drug addiction and mental illness. This recovery was partly due to the discovery that these states of being were not the problem but only a symptom of the problem, the problem was within me, and was created through fear. This book is about how I lost that fear and came to trust a higher or inner self, which some may like to call God. The word God will be used throughout this program, and I'd like to point out that it is not necessarily the religious version of God, but more a personal concept of a power greater than ourselves. Today, my religion is Love, the universal oneness of love which is all that is.

My recovery began with a profound spiritual experience which lasted three weeks. This experience left me in no doubt that there was a greater power, at work in the universe, but I had no idea how to trust this power with my life. In the following program I share how I came to realise that all my little fears came under the umbrella of my fear of trusting God, and how, little by little I became one with this power. May you all find this peace.

I would like to mention that this program is loosely based on the twelve steps of Alcoholics Anonymous, but is not representative in any way of the Alcoholics Anonymous program; however I will take this opportunity to sincerely thank them for their wonderful program.

It might be a good idea to read through this program before actually starting on the exercises, you will get a better perspective of where you are headed, and the exercises may be easier to practise.

The second part of this book is made up of inspirations that have come to me over a period of time, often in the early hours of the morning, when I have awakened to quickly write them down before going back to sleep. You might like to try writing your own inspirations down as they come to you.

One last thing before we begin, it is not necessary, but if at all possible, you will find that this program is easier to practise with a friend or an acquaintance, ideally someone with a similar problem, someone who you can share your experiences with, remembering always that each will have their own understanding.

Now before we start, a little about me.

I was born in a small coal mining town west of the Blue Mountains in NSW. There I trained as a fitter and Turner at the Lithgow Small arms factory. At the completion of my apprenticeship I began my travels around the world as an engineer and later around Australia as a fisherman and crayfish and pearl shell diver. I spent quite a lot of time in northern Australia and the Torres Straights, where I had a couple of relationships which produced three children.

My life from the age of seventeen was plagued by alcoholism, drug addiction and gambling, steadily progressing to hospital detox and rehabilitation centres, and at the age of forty two, finally culminating in mental health problems and suicidal thoughts. A profound spiritual experience or as some call it a psychic change set me on the path to recovery. Through this change I discovered the truth in many of the eastern traditions, and this truth led me to a diploma in traditional Chinese medicine 'Acupuncture.' I then obtained certificates in Shiatsu massage, Iridology, and later I became a certified drug and alcohol counsellor, and am now a qualified Reiki Master. As I progressed into my spiritual reality I discovered that although these traditions were very helpful, they were only part of a greater tradition which is the source of all that is.

The following program is an attempt by me to share this wonderful journey in the hope others may find the peace that I now experience, and in turn, share this with those we know who are suffering.

Ronald Russell

Part One

The NO DIET, DIET

Doesn't make sense? It will.

Michelangelo, when asked how he created his famous masterpiece, the sculpture of David, replied. 'The form was already in the stone, I only had to remove the material from around the statue.' It is the same with us. We are perfect beings, you only have to look inside to find the REAL you.

Let us first look at how the world eating disorders have become one of the greatest threats to mankind, it all began when the word DIET became a 'FAD'. We began to diet to lose weight, to gain weight, to change our shape, to feel better about ourselves, and then the health industry took over with diet pills, diet formulas, weight loss programs etc. Now the food industry have jumped on the band wagon with diet milk, diet drinks, diet ice cream, jams, cheese, cakes etc., etc., etc. I even used the DIET word twice in our heading to gain your attention. What this boils down to is that if you want to diet you are probably not happy with yourself as you are, or, you may be afraid of losing what you have now. (FEAR). Either way we are afraid that we aren't, or won't be loved. This means we don't love ourselves.

You may wonder why I put so much emphasis on diet when this is a spiritual program.

"All that we are is the result of what we have thought." Buddha.

Our thoughts tell our minds how to create our body. It is not only calories that cause us to put on weight. It is our thoughts which play a large part in every part of our evolution. When we eat a diet sweet, we aren't eating many calories, but our mind is telling our body that we are eating something sweet and the sweet craving is set in motion, this leads us to the HIDDEN sugars in carbohydrates, and the carbohydrate addiction is possibly the greatest addiction we have in today's world.

It is the same with other addictions as well, take alcohol for example; science can tell us how alcohol is processed in the body, but not in the mind. Many alcoholics have tried to abstain from alcohol by drinking a non-alcoholic alternative, only to find that the mind still thinks it is drinking and before long the real thing is replacing the pseudo drink. With drugs it is the same, I personally have been affected by a pseudo mind altering drug, to the extent that I believed that I was stoned. This pseudo, or placebo effect is often used medically when a pseudo drug is given to patients. Many recover from their illness when the mind is tricked into believing it is receiving the correct medication. It is the same with electronic cigarettes; yes they are breaking the nicotine addiction but not the smoking habit, often leading to the person picking up nicotine through the smoking habit. Gambling is similar, many who believe they are addicted to gambling, are only addicted to poker machines, they couldn't be bothered putting two cents on a football match or race horse. The bells and whistles and flashing lights are the attraction; they can sit in front of a poker machine for hours, completely immersed in another world totally hidden away from this sometimes painful world of reality. They too can fool their mind, by playing computer games, thinking they have broken the habit of the pokies, unfortunately when they enter an area where the pokies are calling with their bells and whistles they find there is no resistance in the mind because it has been fed on the pseudo poker machine called computer games.

When we look at all the above it is not difficult to see how our addictions are only a symptom of our problems, the problem is within us.

This program will show you how to create your own Michelangelo masterpiece which already exists within.

It has always been there. It will only take the desire and willingness to allow us to guide you on the journey from your thoughts to the real you. Remember, you have already been created; NOW see who you REALLY are.

"You do not have a soul; you are a soul, who has a body."

This program is applicable to those who suffer with Alcoholism, Drug addiction, Gambling, Depression, Anxiety, Weight Loss, Grief, Uncontrolled Emotions and a range of other debilitating conditions.

Welcome to our Workshop.

THE PROGRAM

This first exercise may seem a little difficult at the start, but we will come back to it along the way. Please take your time with this exercise.

Start by finding a quiet place where you won't be disturbed, picture in your mind an image of a person you admire above all else. Think of the love, happiness and beauty they exhibit, remembering that these traits come from the inner being. The image may be of an actor, whose inner and outer beauty you admire, it may be Jesus or Buddha or Mohamed, Mother Teresa might suit you more. It might be a spiritual teacher you know or have seen, or it may be the image of the you that you wish to create, some find a photo of themselves that they like and display this prominently in their home, or a cutting from a magazine. For now the only requirement is that the image is the image you wish to create. Now imagine that person being you and you being that person, in other words, swap identities, so that the you that's imagined has all the traits you admire and wish to create. Hold that picture in your mind until it becomes solid. Practise throughout each day, bringing this image to the fore of your mind. Imagine that you are the great sculptor Michelangelo and you will be making a 3D live image of this picture, and all you have to do is remove the excess material from around it. What will be left is a magnificent masterpiece RE- CREATED by you. REMEMBER, IT HAS ALWAYS BEEN THERE.

It is very important to mention that the person who you are now, or at least who you THINK you are, must be accepted as you are, by you, warts and all. A good way to do this is to sit quietly and take stock of who you are now, without fear. You may be poor, you may be fat, or thin, you may be suffering from an addiction, or mental illness, the important thing is to be as honest as possible and say to yourself without fear, something like this. "My name is Ronald, and I'm sitting in this chair right now, I know I'm drinking too much, or I am definitely over weight, suffering from anxiety, have trouble leaving the house, have a bad gambling problem or addiction to drugs. Maybe you are sitting in a prison cell, the point is that we must own where we are at in this moment. We can't fix the problem unless we admit and accept we have the problem. Listen to that inner voice, that intuition that is telling you to be honest in this assessment. I would like to point out that it is quite OK to be where you are now, as a matter of fact it is totally necessary to be where you are now, no justifications, no judgements, just exactly as you are. Popeye the cartoon character is continually stating,

"I am what I am, and that's all that I am"

NOW TO WORK

Let us take up the tools and start chipping away at all of the excess material covering our masterpiece. This rubble can only be removed by love, and the knowledge that this jewel already exists. We explained earlier how Fear is preventing us from loving ourselves and now we will see that the material or rubble we have to remove is made up of those fears. F.E.A.R.

False Evidence Appearing Real.

"GOD DOESN'T LIVE IN THE FRIDGE"

The aim of this program is to become aware of what is going on inside that makes us look outside for comfort, actually the whole program is based on this awareness.

How often do we find ourselves standing and looking into the fridge, door open, peering in, and looking for who knows what? Quite often, we find ourselves at the fridge just after having eaten a full meal, including sweets, we would be hard pressed to eat another mouthful, but for some reason we think we can fill that empty hole from the fridge. It is not only the fridge we look to, our problem could be called the disease of MORE. We don't seem to be happy with what we have for very long, how many times we have said if only I had a better car, or better Job, or partner, always looking outside to fill that hole inside. That hole which will always be there until we become whole within ourselves.

One definition of insanity is that we keep on repeating our mistakes expecting a different result. How many times have we gone back into the same uncomfortable situation or relationship expecting a different result? "If nothing changes, nothing changes." When we are whole within ourselves we are not looking outside for fulfilment and so can accept any situation as it is, and either stay in it or move out as we see fit without fear, you see, it is the fear that is holding us to these unwholesome choices, because we aren't whole within, we feel we need something else to fix us up. Remember…"God doesn't live in the fridge."

The empty hole I'm talking about is really our distance from God; we are searching for something from outside to fill that void. When I mention God in this program, I'm not necessarily talking about the religious idea of God, more that inner jewel we all have experienced at some time or another, that intuition from deep inside that lets us know if something is wrong. We all have some sort of an understanding that there is something greater than our human self organising everything, even if it is only our inner self or higher self. I sometimes call this power, AWARENESS. Our problem is that we don't trust this awareness. Don't worry about not being able to describe whatever it is, all the greatest spiritual teachers tell us that the TAO (GOD) that can be explained is not the eternal TAO. A very good friend calls it the 'Unwordable' meaning that which cannot be explained by words.

Fear is the absence of love, and fear cannot exist in the presence of love, so we realise that LOVE IS LETTING GO OF FEAR and the rubble we have to remove is fear, which is not real. Your job now is to keep your image in mind throughout the days, realising that what you don't see in the picture doesn't really exist.

Following are a list of words which are to be removed from your thoughts and vocabulary. When I say remove them I don't mean fight against them, more like, letting them go, as we become aware that we are using these negative words we automatically allow them to slip out of use, more and more you will notice that not just you, but many around you will be using these words, and as you do, you will become aware of their negative power. This is a good time to look for the good in all things, remembering not to create a craving for only the good, but to realise that we wouldn't realise the good if we didn't have the bad to compare it to.

These are some of the negative words which tend to put us down creating fear. The first is can't, followed by, impossible, try, limitation, but, difficult, ought to, should, shouldn't, doubt, if only, hate, or any words or sentences that might put you down in any way. Another little tip; when we notice ourselves using words like strive for, or fight for, change your thinking to ALLOW, allow things to come into your life rather than putting pressure on yourself by fighting or striving. We are not trying to change who we are, we are letting go of who we are not, and we do this through awareness. Oh I know you are feeling that if I don't strive or fight for something I will never get it, no blame, this is part of the fear we have learnt to accept as fact. In reality, or if you like in Gods world, abundance is everywhere, and it is only by acceptance and awareness that we will allow ourselves to be in the right place at the right time to accept this abundance.

From now on it is all positive, we will RE- DISCOVER the real you, but first we have to find out what type of fears created the unreal you.

YOU CREATED THEM, ONLY YOU CAN DISOLVE THEM

We will begin with pen and pad. Taking our time, we write down how we ourselves, or others, have been, or are still being, affected by these fears or negative thinking. FEAR AND EGO WALK HAND IN HAND, one can't exist without the other.

Let's start with Resentments, probably the cause of the majority of our fear, then jealousy, self pity, envy, laziness, criticising, dishonesty, impatience, hate, arrogance, procrastination, insincerity, pride, greed, self condemning, self justification. What about our sex relations, how have we mishandled these? What makes me feel uncomfortable? What has that to do with me? Have any of the above defects caused us to harm others? Remember, we can't blame the other person. This part must be done with complete honesty.

WRITE IT DOWN

These fears which are caused by our ego could be called (sins) but sin in the time it was used in religious texts, was an archery term, used to describe the arrow missing the target or mark. This being the case, having missed the mark, we can try again taking a better aim while being aware of the reasons why we missed before.

NO BLAME

Notice I mentioned awareness again, if we aren't aware of our defects, then it stands to reason that we can do nothing about them, and they will continue to cause us trouble until such time as we do become aware of them. Actually, in my book, awareness is the higher power which is behind the intuition, or gut instinct I referred to earlier.

Let's look at resentments. Some call them RE-sent thoughts, thoughts that keep coming back time after time, haunting us, stealing our peace, creating endless sleepless nights. We spend countless hours planning how to get even, even going as far as planning murder, with the thought "If only I could get away with it." Others liken it to taking poison and hoping the person whom we hold the resentment against will die, that's how much harm resentments can cause. Our immune system crashes, and we find ourselves coming down with all kinds of illnesses, and it all comes from blaming someone or something outside of ourselves, we can't see yet, that the problem 'is within me.'

This again comes back to the fear that if this person is not punished they will keep on doing the same thing, as with all fears we feel we must control the situation, and usually, if not always, the problem is in the past and we cannot control the past, likewise thinking they might do it again is like controlling the future. We have no idea what the future will bring. Through this program we will come to realise that the only thing we can control is ourselves in this moment, and what others do is none of our business. There is another saying I like "There are no mistakes in Gods' world." This is a black and white statement, no shades of grey, if you believe it, then live it, if not, let it go, either way, NO blame.

Then there's the "If only." If only they would do it the way I would do it, If only I was in charge of the country we wouldn't be in this trouble. I'm upset now because they didn't do it my way, and I'm sure it will lead to trouble in the future. Can you see how this constant negative thinking leads us away from inner peace?

Jesus, one of the great masters said;

"Forgive them for they know not what they do."

To me, that means that the resentment and anger they were showing towards Jesus on the cross was eating away at them and they were doing themselves more damage than they realised.

Jealousy, guilt and all of the other defects are to be written down without justification, remembering to mention who we harmed through our practise of these defects. Hopefully we will discover that all of these defects, if carried through to the end, were realised through fear. We will get to see how these defects affect our self esteem, or our financial security, and eat away at our confidence, creating even more fear.

If we have been honest with this list we would have quite a few pages. As mentioned before, these negative traits or defects of character are the rubble or stone which has to be removed before we find the real masterpiece. It is said, "a problem shared, is a problem halved" and you can't really have half a problem. Anyway, as I see it, a problem is only a problem if you call it a problem; otherwise it is just, life as it is. If we don't call it a problem, we don't have a problem. It's as simple as that. This is the type of thinking we would like to encourage;

ACCEPT LIFE AS IT IS, NOT AS WE WOULD LIKE IT TO BE

Now might be a good time to remember that we are becoming aware as to why we think our answer lies in the fridge. As we become aware of a few realities, we become uncomfortable within ourselves, we are not used to being honest about these things and have usually hidden away or tried to escape by our chosen addiction, anything to fill that hole created by fear.

Our solution then is to share with (Tell) another human being and the God of your understanding, all of these negative defects. This will require a great deal of HUMILITY, which is the 'destroyer' of EGO or FEAR. (Oh, and by the way, a good definition of humility is to understand that there is a little bit of Hitler and a little bit of Jesus in us all.) We find someone we can trust completely, it may be a very close friend, some feel comfortable with a priest, minister or spiritual teacher, some find separate people for separate issues. This might be the first time you have ever trusted anyone. It will become the keystone to trusting your higher power in the future. These steps are not to clean up your old life, but to create a platform on which to start a brand new life, completely free of the old.

Freedom from fear is our goal here, so we must be painfully honest. Whoever we choose, we can leave nothing behind. From this cleansing, we begin our journey into a new and healthy life. This may feel daunting, but remember, many before you have cleared their rubble to find their Michelangelo masterpiece. Having done this we sit quietly and check that we have left nothing behind, and if satisfied, keeping only the list of people we have harmed, we set the list on fire and watch as our defects (fears) go up in smoke to the universe, although some like to hold onto this list of defects to see where they have come from.

It is important now to have some quiet time, where we can reflect on where we are at in this moment, asking ourselves whether we really want to be free of all these defects. One defect many have trouble leaving behind is anger, we feel anger is sometimes justifiable, others use it as a means of control, but in this program, we hope to replace anger with love, kindness and compassion.

The next and probably the most important step is to realise that we can live our life without the control we used these fears for. We learn to trust that everything is as it is, and trust that it will be alright. This means to let go of our personal control and trust the inner or higher self to look after things, a very big step for some. Remember when we were sitting on a chair at the beginning of this program? We saw ourselves honestly as we were then, our best thinking, our best control got us to that point. Now we have the chance to hand over the reins, and allow a power greater than ourselves to bring us through recovery to a brand new life.

Many call this inner self their intuition; it is that gut instinct, the knowing that something is right or wrong. If we stay still we can ask this inner voice whether we are on the right path or not. We could call it God, or the Master, I often ask the question "What would the Master do? Then sit quietly and the answer comes, and I intuitively know that it is the right answer.

We are almost in view of the real jewel inside. All that is remaining is to clean up the mess we have made, this means to make amends to those on the list who we have harmed, as long as in so doing we don't harm them or others again. We remember that we are making amends for the harm we caused to others which cannot be justified by the harm they may have caused us. We only clean our side of the fence, what they may have done has nothing to do with us. Common sense must be used here, it would not be wise or helpful if we were to admit to something that would land us in jail, or have us physically harmed in any way. Some people may not be reached, others we may have trouble making amends to just now, and the right attitude is to have the intention to make amends when the right time appears. Our changed behaviour and attitude may be enough for others. No more looking over our shoulders, we will be able to walk free wherever we wish to go as long as we practise this step to the best of our ability.

Now to begin the inner journey to whom we really are.

Find a quiet place to sit where you won't be disturbed for around 30 minutes. Turn your phone, radio, TV, etc., off. Sit in as comfortable a position as possible, back straight and upright. This step may be done while lying down, the benefits are not as good and you may fall asleep. Now read this next paragraph and remember what you must do.

Gently close your eyes and feel your breath entering your body, feel your stomach rising and falling with each breath, breath normally and naturally, continue observing your breath and stomach rising and falling, rising and falling for a minute or two, (this time can be increased with practise). If your mind drifts away from your breath and you start to think about past or future, recognise this by saying softly to yourself, "thinking, thinking, no blame this is how it is," then gently bring your mind back to your breath. Now bring to mind someone or something that you have felt love for, or have received love from, the unconditional love that you know comes from, or enters into your heart, for some, this may be the love a mother has for her child, others, their dog, or cat, it is possible to do this exercise while stroking a purring cat or loving dog, love is universal. As it states in the Desiderata;

"You are a child of the universe, no less than the trees and stars,"

This exercise could be done while hugging a tree if you felt comfortable with that. Feel love flowing from the inner you. Stay with this love for 5 minutes increasing to 20 minutes down the track. Practise at least once each day preferably in the morning before your day gets hectic. Whenever you find your mind wandering, no blame, just calmly bring it back to your breath for a while, and then continue on as before.

Some may not be able to feel this love at first, it doesn't matter, it is as it is, you are probably looking for it, just accept the relaxing feeling as love, you see, we all have a preconceived idea of what love is, this is our mistake, just trust that, if you are able to practise this program in any way, you are practising in love, you will understand this more as time goes by.

If you get a chance, take a walk into the bush or forest, sit quietly and become one with the forest, listen to the sounds of the forest, the birds, the wind through the branches, maybe the distant sound of a vehicle, a small animal scurrying by, do not concentrate on any particular sound, but listen to the harmony of them all together, this is the harmony of love, allow yourself to be as one within this harmony, this is the inner jewel you really are, no longer separate, but one in harmony with all that is. That is what the word Namaste' means, we are one. Have you ever sat quietly with your dog, no words, then for no reason your eyes meet and you find yourself looking into the bottomless depths of those wonderful brown eyes, nothing else exists in that moment, now you are living in love. You will never lose these moments, one only has to be still and remember them to be there again, in times of turmoil, be still and know that you are this love.

We were created as love and we can only give what we have. This exercise will develop the love we have inside us. We will be able to give to all, realising, that we really ARE the love we are giving. Following are some different forms love can take.—Generosity, kindness, Empathy, Humility, Modesty, Patience, Forgiveness, Trust, Courage, Wisdom, Sincerity, Compassion, Joy, Happiness. You may like to add to this list. "We become what we practise". The jewel of love is our inner being or our Michelangelo masterpiece waiting to be uncovered, the more we recognise and practise these love traits, the closer is our masterpiece to being 'Re-discovered.'

What does our Michelangelo Masterpiece look like?

- YOU ALREADY KNOW.- YOU HAVE ALWAYS KNOWN-

This next exercise is to be practised whenever you get a spare moment. While waiting for a bus, while stopped at traffic lights, or in a traffic jam, while waiting for an appointment, walking to shops, along a beach, going to bed or sleep, anywhere, anytime. Think of the person you admire above all else, think of the love traits they exhibit. It may be Jesus, or Buddha, or Mohamed, or it may be Nelson Mandela, or Ghandi, or Mother Teresa, no doubt you have your own vision. Now, imagine that person being you, and you being that person, more importantly, imagine how you would look, act and feel, if you were that person, feel the feelings of joy and happiness, experience the love, SEE the beauty. This is YOUR inner Michelangelo Masterpiece. This is the REAL YOU. Practise these exercises with gentle compassion toward yourself and you will become your inner jewel.

I personally use Jesus as my mind, or meditation mentor, I am not necessarily a Christian. As I have stated before, my religion is love, and I find that Jesus exhibits all the qualities I wish to recognise within. When in trouble I find myself asking, what would the master do? If you would like to take meditation further I would suggest you look up a Buddhist technique at a Vipassana meditation retreat. These are ten day silent retreats, focussing on mindfulness, and are run by volunteers. Payment is by donation after one has completed the ten days.

I have a number of meditation techniques on You Tube. If you wish to listen to them search for

'ronald russell video 39.' It should reveal all the videos of mine.

There are other mindfulness videos there which are excellent to sit and meditate with.

Each day for thirty minutes, find time to meditate, becoming consciously aware of your oneness with a God of your understanding. My favourite words are ALLOW and HARMONY, I see the harmony of all that is, the whole universe working together as it should, my job is to allow myself to be a part of that harmony, and not separate as I was before. This could be called a spiritual awakening. Awakening to the fact that I am not a separate entity any longer, but one with the universe, trusting that the universe is evolving as it is, and as long as I allow myself to evolve with it, I will know peace.

Notice that I used the words ALLOW and HARMONY, they are words which resonate with me, everyone has one or two words that resonate with them, I chose them from a list of positive words while meditating, looking at them in hindsight they seem to be words that I most needed in life. I could never allow anything to happen of its own accord or in its own time, I was always striving for some goal or another, always causing stress by trying to make things happen my way. Today, with trust in God and the knowledge that 'it will be alright,' I'm able to allow life to happen as it is.

Similarly with harmony, everything is as it is. When I see the word Harmony I see the world as it really is, we can't have highs without lows, joy without sadness, death without life, mountains without valleys, and it's all happening at once in harmony, again the quote, "There are no mistakes in Gods world." And I'm right there smack bang in the middle, allowing myself to be guided, like everything else, by that invisible force called awareness or Love.

Now, something for the mechanical or biological mind to chew on. Well over two thousand years ago, enlightened persons were sharing the secret with us that we were much more than we thought we were. They were telling us that we were part of the universe, and that the universe is within us, since then there have been many more experiencing this phenomenon. Today, with the help of our miraculous new scientific instruments, and magnifying lenses, we are able to literally see, what was until recently, only experienced.

Quantum science or Quantum mechanics has opened up a brand new world for those interested in the mechanics of spirituality, allowing us to see how everything works in harmony. This is too much for this simple program, but for those who want a little food to chew on, that doesn't come from the fridge, I'll pass this on.

If we think of the body as being made up of millions of cells, and we think of everything outside of the body as being made up of millions of cells then it stands to reason that as the cellular being, we are similar to the outside cellular universe. Oh, I know we, and the universe is made up of much smaller particles, but for now, and for simplicity's sake, let's keep it at the cellular level.

It has been discovered that our cells have what might be called a mind of their own which is in tune with their environment, and can change with the changes in their environment. These cell changes, have an effect on our DNA, and can actually change its performance. The environment the cell lives in, is as far as the body goes, is controlled by us, i.e., The food we eat, the toxins we allow to come in contact with our cells, even our thoughts affect our cells, they are continually picking up signals from their surrounding environment and changing to suit this environment. For example, when we become angry, the cells pick this energy up and because it doesn't enjoy an angry environment makes a change within itself or the DNA so that it can feel comfortable within itself, and before too long, if the anger persists, our whole being becomes infected with anger, the opposite happens with Love.

Now, realising that everything is cellular or atomic if you wish, even the atmosphere around us, then it is not hard to imagine us to be similar to a cell in the greater body of the universe, and just as the cells inside our body are affected by changes in our internal environment, and our minds, so too are we affected by the outer universe or the "Mind of God "as some would call it.

If we look at it this way, each cell is in touch at some level with every cell in the universe and is being affected in some way or another depending on the environment it is exposed to. This then goes a long way to explaining the wars and suffering that we all see happening throughout our world.

Every moment millions of cells are dying because of old age and war going on continuously within our body environment, this has to happen to maintain harmony within the body, some cells are attacking harmful cells and killing them others are complementing cells, and as long as the environment is healthy, harmony is maintained.

It is no different in the bigger picture, animals kill and eat other animals, trees take in carbon dioxide and give out oxygen, things come into being only to pass away again, nothing is static, all is moving in harmony, and just as the wars within bring about a balance in line with the environment, so to do the wars in the bigger picture bring about a similar balance.

"As it is within, so it is without'

We are a product of our environment, as we destroy our environment, we destroy ourselves, but remember, this works both ways, as we improve our environment we improve ourselves, This is a very important fact to remember when we are recovering from our 'dis- ease', We must be aware of the company we are keeping in recovery,

"Man who sleeps with dogs wakes up with fleas."

Each separate cell within our body has its own 'mem-brain' which is consciously aware of its environment, just as we have a brain which is aware of its environment, but not always consciously. This is why quiet times are so important, to bring our conscious mind in harmony with our subconscious, if we don't have this time, we find our conscious mind is going off in its own direction, completely blind to the way real life is actually supposed to happen, or actually is happening.

Humans and everything else react in the same way as the cells which make our bodies up, the trick is to recognise that these inner cells don't stop at our skin, they continue past our outer skin and on into the universe, all working harmoniously together. There is no line where our skin stops and the universe begins, IT IS ALL ONE.

If trillions of cells can live in harmony within the universe of our bodies, maybe the small amount of eight billion humans can learn to live in harmony with all that is.

It is not hard to see that if we want harmony within our body we have to create a harmonious environment for our cells to live in, and as cells, in the bigger picture, we have to create a harmonious environment for all to live in. There is something larger than all of this in which all and nothing lives, there are many names for this, some call it the Tao, others call it the mind of God, and still others call it Awareness, myself, I call it Love, and to be able to live in the harmony of this love is the ultimate way of being.

I will leave this here now, but if your appetite was whetted then I suggest you read;

"The Wisdom of Your Cells" By Bruce H Lipton, PhD

"Ageless Body Timeless Mind" By Deepak Chopra,

Following are a list of positive words you might like to meditate on, one will resonate with you, watch this word while you meditate, it may stay in view for a while then disappear, then come back again, if it doesn't no worries, it will eventually, this word will become a reminder of what you must do to be as one with all that is. You will find yourself seeing this word at any time of the day or night reminding you that you are one with God or Love.

THE WORDS

Silent, calm, still, joy, happy, peace, ecstasy, bliss, allow, stop, slowdown, quiet, love, rest. No doubt you can find more. Find your word and make it your peace word.

Maintenance

It is not up to us to tell you what to do, or what to, or not to eat, however we will offer a few tips.

1—Love your food as you love your body.

2—Eat "real" food, as did our great grandparents and those before them.

3—Stay well away from diet, salty, fat or sugar reduced foods.

4—It is best to eat complex carbohydrates like (oats and whole grains.) Limit their intake.

5—Avoid simple and hidden sugars. Find out more about these sugars.

6—Take the time to find out what the benefits of 'real' foods are, as you progress through this program, you will know intuitively the correct food to eat.

7—Go for a comfortable walk once or twice each day, taking in and being grateful for your surroundings.

8—Realise that you are a "Child of the Universe."

9—As we retire at night, we look back over our day, if we have wronged ourselves or others in any way, we accept we were wrong and make amends wherever possible.

> You are well on your way to becoming the real you. It is your responsibility to share what you have learned.

"LOVE ATTRACTS LOVE" "TO GIVE IS TO RECIEVE"

There are many ways to share this.

You could tell a friend about this program, you might like to create a Face book page, I have one called Living in Love" Best of all, through the social media pages you could arrange to get together once or twice a week with others in your community for face to face meetings or discussion groups where love and hugs are exchanged.

Church halls and similar venues attract a very reasonable rental for this type of activity, or maybe meet in a cafe, all that is needed is use of a toilet and tea and coffee making facilities. Or you could join one of the groups mentioned below.

You may have noticed that throughout this program we have used the word WE, suggesting that you are supported by all through love. YOU ARE NOT ALONE.

"You are a child of the universe, no less than the trees and stars; you have a right to be here. And whether or not it is clear to you, no doubt the universe is unfolding as it should. With all its sham, drudgery and broken dreams, it is still a beautiful world. Be careful. Strive to be happy."(Desiderata,)

This program is a product of the universe. You are now responsible for those who come after you. Just as you are finding the real you, we can find the real world hidden under its fear.

Recommended readings. ---

A Return to Love-------Marianne Williamson

There is a spiritual solution to every problem. -----Wayne W Dyer

A deep breath of life--- Alan Cohen

Seven Spiritual laws to Success---Deepak Chopra

Power of Now------Eckhart Tolle

The Profit -----------Kalhil Gibran

The Untethered Soul-----Michael A Singer

The Voice of Knowledge' -----Don Miguel Ruiz

Loving what is-----Byron Katie

Sadhana; The Realization of Life-----Rabindranth Tagore

You might like to choose any book by the above authors. Advanced readers,---'A course in miracles' Original edition, by ----Helen Schueman. I would suggest that you start with the workbook. This workbook is also available free in text and audio via the internet.

If you feel you may have other problems or need more help, there are many programs in the community which are compatible with this program, and they may be contacted via the Net. e.g., Alcoholics Anonymous--- Narcotics Anonymous----Gamblers Anonymous----Overeaters Anonymous, and many more. Many with Emotional – Physical and Spiritual problems have found relief in these programs.

In conclusion I would like to point out that the awareness you have discovered through this program will allow you to recognise that the next time you are peering into the fridge, or looking outside for something to make you feel whole, that God doesn't live in the fridge, He lives in you and you in Him. We are one.

NAMASTE'

Part Two

INSPIRATIONS

Sitting quietly, listening to a lonely dove calling for its mate in the far off distance;
There's a little Willie Wag Tail flitting about catching invisible insects.
A "Will O'the Wisp" type breeze, here one moment, gone the next.
Carrying sounds from far away, then, as soon as they are heard, silent again;
Contemplating the clouds silently sailing across the azure sky, sails billowing like some ghostly ships,
Only to disappear behind the distant headland glistening green on the horizon.
Then the wonderful realization, all this is happening now.
This is not some magical dream, or fancied wishful thought.
All around is harmony.....It is here now.....Is there more?
I don't know.....This is more than enough for now,

Ronald Russell   Namaste'

NAMASTE'

*I honour the place in you
in which the entire universe dwells
I honour the place in you
which is of love, of truth, of light,
and of peace.
When you are in that place in you
and I am in that place in me,
WE ARE ONE*

Allow Love

If we are honest with ourselves, we find very few of us want to hurt others. The inner us wants to be loving kind and compassionate. It is only when fear drops its veil over us that we lose the awareness of love. We become whatever energy we are using, If we are using anger, jealousy, or hatred to fight the fear, then we become that energy, every cell joins forces to fight fear, and is infected with the same hurtful energies. It is when we realise the existence of the deep eternal love within which does not fight or strive for its existence that we become aware of the futility in fighting something outside of this love.

I love the saying

"Fear knocked, Love answered.

No one was there"

Ronald Russell   Namaste'

It begins with me

For too long have I looked outside.
If you are into meditation and or contemplation,
I have one for you.

'The world changes through me'
When I look on the world with fear,
I won't see peace.
It is only when I recognise myself
as pure unconditional love,
Will I see the world in the same way.
While I am fighting in any way,
against anything,
I am fighting against peace.
As I forgive myself I forgive the world.
There is no separation in love.

Ronald Russell   Namaste'

The Gift

*In the darkest night,
we find the brightest light. There is always a gift.
No matter how dark life becomes,
How long the hell seems to last,
Know and trust that this too will pass,
and as it does the gift will be revealed.
Search for the gift in your sadness.
There is always a gift.*

Ronald Russell   Namaste'

Allowing God to do for us
that which we cannot do for ourselves.
To do without doing.
Allowing Harmony.
Not my will but thine be done.
Have you ever noticed that when a child is hurt.
There is an instant response
from us as the observer to pick them up.
Have you noticed that when someone is suffering,
our heart opens with love toward them.
This kindness and love
are not energies from outside ourselves,
but that which everything is, finding its own level.
As we lose fear and allow ourselves to be what we really are,
we find ourselves loving without loving,
giving without giving, doing without doing.
You see. it's just a matter of BEing.
It is in the stillness of BEing that I know I Am.

Ronald Russell   Namaste'

Thinking Differently

There's a little bit of broken in us all.
This is a part of the human condition.
IT is 0nly with the realization and acceptance of this condition that I see the suffering of self.
Who am I ???
Who stands outside of self and witnesses this human condition,
Am I God ???
There is no time.
Just a oneness with everything and nothing.
I know I am not the suffering that I am observing.
So much joy, happiness, oneness, Love.
Yes Love, I am Love.

Ronald Russell   Namaste'

Its a matter of Being

Life is like chasing moonbeams.
Seems like an impossible task,
but if you stay very quiet and still,
you may become one.

Ronald Russell   Namaste'

Shhhhh Listen

What is it that lives between the words?
In the pauses after the comma and full stop.
In the silence,
between the incoming and outgoing breath.
Could it be the quiet,
where wisdom is born?

Ronald Russell   Namaste'

Dawn is just starting to colour the sky with its pearly hue, I'm up early this morning quietly sitting and allowing the harmony of all that is flow throughout. I feel the cool fresh breeze on my bare arms and legs; I smell the freshness that this breeze brings from the fields along the nearby river. The early birds are starting their song and in the distance a rain bird calls its mate, it will probably rain in three days, it is probably right, I notice the ants hurriedly moving to higher ground, Sonny Boy the Golden Labrador lazily wanders over, licks at my hand to let me know he is here, I look down into the depths of the most loving golden brown eyes, for a moment we connect, we are one, the moment passes but is not lost, he is happy to settle at my feet, no sound, no words just a silent knowing that in this moment all is as it should be, my heart is singing and I know we are living in love and harmony with all that is.

Ronald Russell   Namaste'

The sadness has settled over me again as I think of you, I separate again from love and ask, why? It has been a long while since we lived, laughed and cried in loving friendship, the intimate exchanges of unconditional love and trust. Oh, I know that bond still exists, but, since your addiction has surfaced, it has been lost behind a veil of ever darkening fear. As your flame dies, so too does mine as I watch you getting further away from who you really are. I feel in my heart that you are separating from that ever healing love. Then, out of the blue, a message, you seem bright and positive, my heart starts to sing, you are excited and want to talk, then, nothing. The sadness settles again, this is not the first time, Many times I see that bright flame that is you, separate from the fire and slowly die to a smouldering smoking darkness, but there has always been that small spark of life, and every now and then, it bursts into that brilliant flame of love and light. My heart is singing again. But I know the darkness you live in, and the flame dies to a smoulder once again, the sadness sets in. Too many have I seen go away like this. Then another message and it starts again, because I know that with love in our heart, we can live through this.

Living in Love with you eternally.

- HOME -

To enter into this place of trust.
This place where I see the utter uselessness of control.
To see the whole picture, but only work on one part of it.
To see life and death as one.
To realise that I am always doing my best with what I have in this moment.
To realise I will do what I will do and nothing will alter that.
To understand nothing I have done or will do is either good or bad, it just is.
To understand that each past experience has brought me to this moment now.
To understand I can't strive for love and trust, but can allow them to enter my life.
To realise that in this moment I am exactly where I am supposed to be and everything is as it is.
To know that when I'm afraid I'm afraid and that's ok too.
To know the everything and nothingness of love, and that wisdom is experience learned.
When I know all this __I am Home,

Living in Love -----Namaste'

Letter to a friend

I do trust you completely my friend, no that's not totally correct, I trust God completely and I know that what is happening is happening, I found this trust in another's death, I know it has nothing to do with me, yes fears arise but are quickly forgotten in trust. Do any of us know or plan our journey? Does the grass seed blown by the wind choose its landing? We are players on the stage of life in a play that has already been written, and I can only play my part to the best of my ability, for the final curtain has already fallen in the timeless realm of eternity. All is as it is. Live in Love my wonderful friend, Live in Love

Ronald Russell   Namaste'

Letter

Thank you my friend for the kind words, we are all in here trying to do the best we can with what we have.... Sometimes I look at it as if we're climbing a high mountain, all helping each other up over difficult obstacles, we have many different talents, and when we're working as a group we're able to use those talents to the advantage of all.... That's why we have to be honest with who we are. "I am what I am and that's all that I am." (Popeye). If we're wearing a mask and trying to be something we're not, the whole team may fall, At the same time, we must recognise others failings, not to judge them but to stand beside them ready with help if needed. We need a unified effort if we are to reach the top. From where I stand, my friend, you are in a good place and are playing your part well.

Living in Love with you today.

Ronald Russell Namaste

It's not all about me

How many of us feel uncomfortable being around, or talking intimately with those less fortunate than us, those with a disability of sorts, or even those who we may judge as, God help me, being below us.
I have found that when I forget myself in these relationships and take an honest interest in whoever I'm relating to, they become the centre of interest and not me. I have to stop thinking how "I" can arrange the situation, and just be in the situation, going along with it as it is, or as it unfolds.

Ronald Russell   Namaste'

This is what human is

I have experienced the darkness and despair, and the fear this brings.
I have experienced the light and joy and the love this brings.
And this is alright,
for this is what human is.
I am not my name, or photo on the wall,
nor am I a cut out cardboard figure where my body finishes at the edge.
My body does not end at this bag of skin filled with flesh and bones.
No, I am much more than these.
I am the air we breathe, the food we eat, the water we drink. I am the earth we walk on,
The stars and the darkness and the light.
But I am more than this,
I am you and you are me, and we are love.
And this is alright,
for this is what human is.

Ronald Russell   Namaste'

Waves

*As the wave is part of the ocean,
and the ocean is all of the wave,
I am a part of God
and God is all of me.
It's easy to believe we are waves
and forget we are also the ocean.*

Namaste'

One

*We walk by them every day,
sit next to them on public transport,
but we don't see them,
and when we do see them, we are afraid.
You see, they are not like us, not well dressed,
possibly unwashed,
we don't see them laughing and joking with their friends.
There is something sad about his picture,
Maybe, just maybe,
we could find just a little courage,
just a little time for a friendly word,
lend a compassionate ear,
or kindly smile,
sometimes that is enough.
No, not for them,
but for us to realise the power of love within.
You see, we really are one,*

Ronald Russell   Namaste'

Peace

Peace comes to the individual.
Not through good overcoming bad,
but by realizing and accepting
good and bad,
life and death,
are necessary
for the harmony of the universe

Ronald Russell

The Search

I searched the world for my God to find,
He was never in front, or ever behind.
And then one day while on my knee,
I found my God inside of me,
with open heart I then did see,
a brand new world in front of me.
A dazzling glow of energy,
and all I see, became all of me.

Ronald Russell   Namaste'

Separate no longer

*As we feel the pain of separation,
we are reminded that it is only our physical self
which experiences this sensation.
If we can quiet our minds,
we once again experience the equanimity
which allows us to live in the love
where fear and pain do not exist.
This I call
"Living in Love"*

Ronald Russell   Namaste'

It's a matter of being

Please don't judge me for having a God of my own understanding;
If we are truly honest with ourselves,
we will find each of us have our own concept of what God is or isn't.
This separate concept will continue until we awake from the dream of "Human" and become the oneness of "BEing"

Ronald Russell   Namaste'

WE are created in God's Image

*Why are we always searching outside of ourselves for
that peace and serenity so necessary for a fulfilling life?
Why do we feel we have to "give" kindness, love and
compassion?
When as God's image we are the values of,
tolerance, kindness, compassion, love, etc,
that we credit God as having;
As we learn to love ourselves,
that means to awaken to the love we really are,
then we must realise everyone has that same love,
our job then, as I see it,
is to allow the same love in us to awaken the love in others
simply by being love.
The Buddhist Metta and the prayers of other religions are
simply ways of expanding this love.
Allow the fearful to love.
After all we are all one.*

Ronald Russell   Namaste'

The Gift

The gift of giving is to yourself.
Every time you give compassion, kindness, forgiveness,
every time you give love,
you might realise these things didn't come from outside,
they came from you.
You are these things, you are love.
Just as water flows from a higher to a lower plane,
so love flows from you to those in need.
These realizations coming from a loving act,
to know you ARE Love,
is the greatest gift to you.
Live in this love forever.

Ronald Russell   Namaste'

The Realization

*Having received the gift of the understanding that you are Love,
it's not too much of a stretch to see that everyone else must be the same, but what is Love?
We can describe it with words like, compassion and kindness, and these are qualities of love.
Qualities are not solid; they are energy, so Love must be that energy.
Energy flows freely in all directions at once,
and there isn't a separate energy for each of us,
it is the one energy called Love.
If the Love in you is the same
as the Love in me we are one.
There can be no separation at this level.*

Ronald Russell   Namaste'

The Awakening

Now that we realise you and I are one in Love,
we start to wonder where the energy originates.
Maybe from one central place, as light from the sun?
Or the centre of the universe?
No it exists everywhere,
and just as it is flowing through you and me,
it must flow through all that is.
You and I and all that is are
'One in Love'

Ronald Russell   Namaste'

The Becoming

*The end of the journey?
No it never was a journey,
more a becoming that which that which we always were.
That which defies description,
the unwordable, the end of Karma,
where everything becomes nothing and nothing is all that
is, a place we can't go, but can be,
a place that is not a place but the
omnipotent, omnipresent inner part of silence
which is eternal Love.*

Ronald Russell   Namaste'

Conclusion

I hope this booklet has helped in some small way with whatever may be ailing you, remember that it is only a signpost on the journey into yourself. I have tried to keep the language as simple as possible, hopefully making it easier to understand this simple program for complicated people. From now on it is up to you, and there are many signposts, the books I have suggested are only a few of the many available.

Always keep an open mind and a loving heart.

Living in Love with you eternally,

Ronald Russell   Namaste'

The music of the heart is love,
and within its harmony,
The whole world sings

The Ronald Russell   Namaste'

GOD

Grant me the Serenity,
To accept the things I cannot Change,
Courage to change the things I can,
And Wisdom to know the difference.
Living in Love with you eternally,

Namaste'

THE END

www.ingramcontent.com/pod-product-compliance
Lightning Source LLC
LaVergne TN
LVHW091533060526
838200LV00036B/595